BOOKED FOR SUCCESS:

Hit Your Marketing Targets Without Losing Your Mind

Jill L. Ferguson

red dog press

For information, contact:

red dog press

red dog press, a division of In Your Face Ink LLC
Glendale, AZ
www.inyourfaceink.com

ISBN: 979-8-9924943-6-5 Hardback
ISBN: 979-8-9924943-7-2 Paperback
ISBN: 979-8-9924943-8-9 ebook

Cover design and interior design by Rick Schank of Purple Couch Creative
Printed in the United States of America
10 9 8 7 6 5 4 3 2 1

Table of Contents

INTRODUCTION
WHY MARKETING MATTERS

Congratulations—you've written a book. You've wrestled with words, survived edits, and perhaps consumed more coffee than you'd like to admit. Typing "The End" might feel like you've crossed the finish line or at least an important stage, but in reality, you've just arrived at the starting gate of another equally important race: getting your book into the hands of readers.

Here's the truth that most of us wish wasn't true: books don't sell themselves. Even beautifully written ones. Even books published by major publishers. According to Bowker's data, more than four million new book titles (including self-published works) are released annually in the United States alone (Bowker, 2021). That means your book is entering a crowded room where everyone is talking at once. The challenge—and the fun—is figuring out how to make your book stand out.

Busting the "If I Write It, They Will Come" Myth

It's tempting to believe that once your book is on Amazon, Barnes & Noble, or tucked onto a local bookstore shelf, readers will magically find it. Unfortunately for all of us authors, that's rarely the case. Think of marketing as giving your book a microphone. Without it, your book is whispering in Madison Square Garden during a Metallica concert. With effective marketing and publicity, people can hear, pay attention, and decide if your story is the one they've been waiting for.

The Author as Marketer

Traditionally-published authors often assume their publishers will handle all the marketing. While it's true that large publishing houses have marketing departments, the resources are usually focused on big-name authors or books with high sales expectations. For debut or midlist authors, or if you are an author working with a hybrid publisher, much of the marketing falls on your shoulders. And if you're self-publishing? Marketing is not optional—it's the engine that drives visibility and sales.

Before you groan and close this book, let me reassure you: marketing doesn't have to be intimidating. In fact, it can be creative, playful, and surprisingly satisfying. Think of it as extending your storytelling—just in different formats and channels. And this book provides a blueprint to do just that, based on my more than twenty years of writing dozens of books and publishing both with traditional publishers and through self-publishing

Marketing Can Be Fun

Do you enjoy chatting with readers, telling stories on social media, or sharing behind-the-scenes glimpses of your writing process? Then you're already marketing, whether you've realized it or not. Marketing isn't about tricking people into buying something they don't want. It's about finding the people who will genuinely love your book and helping them discover it.

Author and marketer Seth Godin describes marketing as "the art of telling a story that resonates with your audience and then spreads" (Godin, 2005). That's exactly what you're already doing as a writer—you're just expanding the audience and the methods.

What This Book Will Do

This guide is here to walk you, step by step, through the strategies that work—without overwhelming you. Each chapter will give you:

1. **Clear explanations** of why a tactic matters.
2. **Examples and mini case studies** of authors who've used it successfully.
3. **Practical exercises** you can apply right away.

By the time you finish, you'll have the tools to:

- Define your "why" as an author.
- Understand and find your readers.
- Build an author brand you enjoy sharing.
- Use online and offline channels strategically.
- Create a sustainable, long-term marketing plan.
- And create a business (or two) based on your books.

Roadmap of the Journey

Here's a quick preview of what's ahead:
- **Chapter 1** will help you clarify your personal "why."
- **Chapter 2** will walk you through identifying and understanding your readers.
- **Chapter 3** focuses on building your author brand.
- **Chapters 4–6** cover online presence, social media, and reviews.
- **Chapters 7–12** dive into publicity, launch strategies, events, ads, and creative approaches.
- **Chapters 13-15** ties everything together by treating your writing career like the business it is and explores the indie or self-publishing landscape.
- **Chapter 16** offers some final words of encouragement.

Finally, we'll end with a 90-day plan to help you put what you've learned into practice immediately.

So grab your notebook, your favorite pen (or your laptop), and let's get your book the audience it deserves.

References:

Bowker. (2021). *Self-Publishing in the United States*, 2021. ProQuest/Bowker.
Godin, S. (2005). *All Marketers Are Liars: The Power of Telling Authentic Stories in a Low-Trust World.* Portfolio.

CHAPTER 1
KNOWING YOUR WHY

Before you print bookmarks, design a website, or send your first tweet, pause. Take a deep breath. Let's ask the question that will shape everything else you do:

Why are you writing and marketing this book?

This might sound obvious. You wrote a book, so of course you want people to read it. But there are deeper layers. Are you hoping to make a living as an author? Do you want to raise awareness about an issue? Are you trying to leave a legacy for your children and grandchildren? Or maybe you simply want to connect with fellow lovers of your genre.

Clarity on your "why" is your North Star. It will guide which marketing strategies you choose, how much time and money you invest, and what success looks like for you.

Defining Success on Your Terms

Many authors feel pressured to define success as hitting *The New York Times* bestseller list or selling 100,000 copies. But the truth is, success looks different for everyone.

- For a business author, success might mean selling enough copies to land speaking gigs.
- For a poet, it might mean a book that resonates deeply with a small community.
- For a memoirist, success might mean sharing a personal story that changes one reader's life.

The key is to avoid letting other people's goals dictate your own. As author Brené Brown notes, "Clarity is kindness" (Brown, 2018). Knowing what matters to you keeps you from chasing every shiny marketing idea and instead helps you focus on the ones that align with your vision.

Throughout this whole book I will share case studies that may serve as inspiration to you. But for some people, depending on where you are in the process, the case studies may feel overwhelming or intimidating. That's why defining success for yourself is so important. Your success may not look like anyone else's. Or maybe one or more of these case studies will give you ideas of what success beyond your wildest dreams could look like.

So, read on, and remember to take everything one step at a time just like you wrote or are writing your book one word or paragraph at a time.

The Power of Purpose

Simon Sinek, in his influential book *Start with Why* (2009), argues that *people don't buy what you do; they buy why you do it.* Applied to books, readers aren't just interested in your plot summary. They're drawn to the passion and purpose behind your writing.

If your "why" is to entertain, inspire, educate, or spark conversations, that message should infuse your marketing. Purpose makes your outreach authentic. Readers can feel it when you're speaking from a place of genuine passion versus when you're trying to check a marketing box.

Common Whys Among Authors
Here are a few motivations authors often identify:

1. **Creative Fulfillment**—Sharing the stories inside you.
2. **Impact**—Changing minds, inspiring hope, or starting dialogue.
3. **Community**—Building relationships with readers and other writers.
4. **Business Growth** or to be seen as the expert you are— Using your book to grow a speaking career, consulting, or teaching.
5. **Legacy**—Leaving something behind for future generations.

It's perfectly fine to have more than one "why." Just be honest with yourself about which one takes priority right now.

How Your "Why" Shapes Marketing
Once you know your purpose, decisions become easier:

- If your "why" is impact, you might focus on schools, libraries, or nonprofits.

- If your "why" is business growth, LinkedIn and professional conferences might be your best marketing channels.
- If your "why" is community, investing in social media groups or reader clubs makes sense.

Without clarity, you risk wasting time and energy on strategies that don't move you toward what really matters to you.

 CASE STUDY:
Angie Thomas and *The Hate U Give*—From Debut to Phenomenon

When Angie Thomas's debut novel *The Hate U Give* (2017) hit shelves, it didn't just launch her career—it sparked a cultural conversation. The book debuted at #1 on *The New York Times* Young Adult Hardcover Bestseller List (and stayed there for more than 80 weeks) and was adapted into a major motion picture within two years. But behind the breakout success is a story of strategic positioning, authentic marketing, and community momentum.

1. Understanding the Market and Audience

Angie Thomas wrote *The Hate U Give* in response to a clear cultural moment: the rise of the Black Lives Matter movement and ongoing national debates about police brutality and systemic racism.

The story follows Starr Carter, a Black teenager who witnesses the police shooting of her best friend. Thomas, who grew up in Jackson, Mississippi, wanted to give young people a character and story that reflected both the pain and resilience of her community.

From the beginning, she understood that:

1. Young Adult readers were hungry for books that reflected *real, relevant issues.*
2. Educators and librarians were actively looking for diverse books to add to classrooms and reading lists.
3. The larger cultural climate was primed for stories tackling systemic injustice.

By writing authentically for her audience, Thomas positioned her debut as both a powerful work of fiction and a book that could make its way into schools, reading groups, and national conversations.

2. Pre-Release Buzz and Marketing

Long before publication, *The Hate U Give* gained traction in the publishing industry.

- **Auction buzz:** The manuscript sparked a bidding war between 13 publishing houses, eventually landing at Balzer + Bray (HarperCollins) with a reported six-figure advance—a huge deal for a debut YA author.
- **Early marketing strategy:** The publisher positioned the novel as both a must-read YA story and a timely cultural text. Advanced reader copies (ARCs) were sent to teachers, librarians, bloggers, and bookstagrammers. This created a grassroots buzz in communities that could advocate for the book at scale.
- **Strategic endorsements:** Blurbs from established authors and early starred reviews (from *Kirkus Reviews* and *Publishers Weekly*) created credibility, signaling that this was not just another debut novel but a cultural event.

3. Community and Grassroots Momentum

One of the most effective parts of *The Hate U Give*'s marketing was how the book spread through community advocates. Librarians and educators championed the novel as an essential classroom text. Teachers built curriculum units around it, and reading groups across the U.S. picked it up. Social media buzz encouraged young readers to share their emotional reactions on Twitter, Tumblr, Instagram, and later TikTok. Angie Thomas actively engaged with readers online, amplifying their voices and making them feel part of the book's journey. And activist organizations connected with the themes of the novel, further pushing the book into conversations beyond the YA community.

By connecting with grassroots readers, Thomas tapped into authentic, word-of-mouth marketing that amplified the publisher's efforts.

4. Mainstream Media and Cultural Relevance

After publication, *The Hate U Give* became a media darling. It received extensive coverage in major outlets (*The New York Times, NPR, The Atlantic*), often positioned as a book that was both timely and necessary. Celebrities like Oprah Winfrey and John Green praised the book, further boosting visibility. And its themes aligned with national conversations on race and justice, making it a frequent recommendation in think pieces, op-eds, and cultural discussions.

The lesson here is when your book aligns with cultural conversations, it can leap beyond book marketing channels into mainstream media.

5. Film Adaptation and Extended Impact

In an unusual move, Fox 2000 optioned *The Hate U Give* for

film adaptation *before the book was even published.* This not only gave the book added prestige during launch but also extended its lifespan years later when the film (starring Amandla Stenberg) released in 2018.

The adaptation created:

- A new wave of publicity, introducing the story to audiences who hadn't read the book.
- Cross-promotion opportunities (new editions with movie tie-in covers, film trailers featuring the book, book clubs revisiting the text).
- Cultural staying power, ensuring the book remained relevant and in circulation beyond the usual "new release" cycle.

6. Business and Author Brand Growth

The success of *The Hate U Give* positioned Angie Thomas as not just an author but a cultural voice. She followed up with *On the Come Up* (2019) and *Concrete Rose* (2021), both of which hit bestseller lists, supported by her established brand and loyal readership. Thomas became a sought-after speaker, invited to conferences, universities, and literary festivals worldwide.

Her books are now standard texts in schools, ensuring long-term sales and cultural impact.

 ## Key Takeaways from Angie Thomas's Marketing Success

1. Cultural Relevance Matters– Books that authentically reflect societal conversations can transcend typical marketing channels.

2. Community Champions Are Essential– Teachers, librarians, and bookstagrammers amplified her book more effectively than ads could.
3. Multi-Channel Strategy Works– From social media engagement to mainstream press, Thomas's book succeeded because it reached readers everywhere.
4. Long-Term Thinking Extends Lifespan– Early film adaptation deals, educational adoption, and sequels ensured her brand didn't fade after one debut.
5. Author Visibility Is Powerful– Thomas's active presence on social media and willingness to engage with readers made her brand relatable and authentic.

Final Lesson: Angie Thomas proves that even debut authors can achieve massive success when their book combines authentic storytelling, community engagement, cultural relevance, and strategic publishing support.

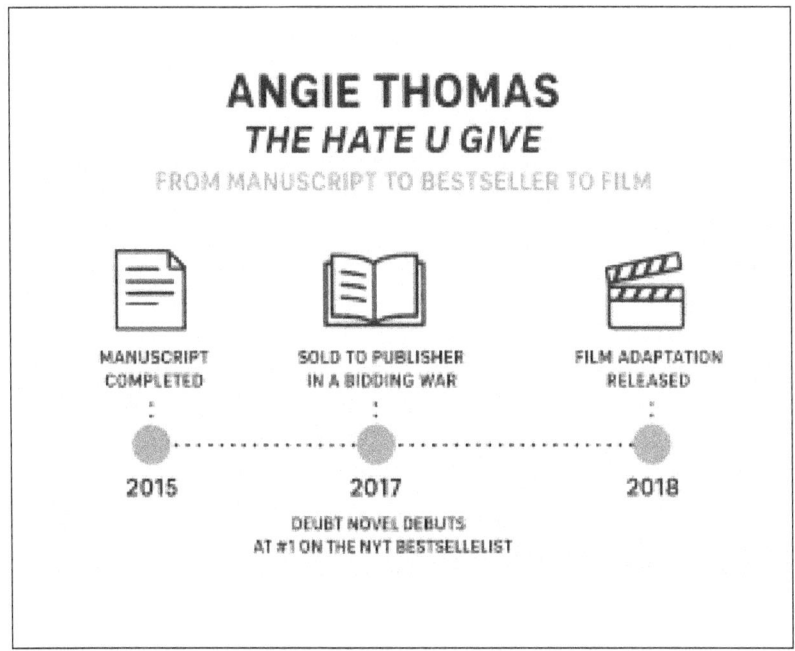

ANGIE THOMAS
THE HATE U GIVE
FROM MANUSCRIPT TO BESTSELLER TO FILM

MANUSCRIPT COMPLETED	SOLD TO PUBLISHER IN A BIDDING WAR	FILM ADAPTATION RELEASED
2015	2017	2018

DEBUT NOVEL DEBUTS
AT #1 ON THE NYT BESTSELLELIST

EXERCISE:
Write Your Author Mission Statement

Take 10 minutes and jot down answers to the following:

1. Why did I write this book?
2. Who do I most want to reach?
3. What do I hope readers feel, learn, or do after finishing it?
4. How will I know I've succeeded?

Now combine your answers into a one-to-two sentence "Author Mission Statement." For example:

"I wrote my cozy mystery series to give readers a comforting escape into small-town life with quirky characters, while also spotlighting the joys of community and friendship. Success for me is building a group of loyal readers who feel at home in my stories."

Keep this mission statement somewhere visible. Refer back to it whenever you feel overwhelmed or distracted by competing marketing advice.

Pitfalls to Avoid

1. Borrowing someone else's why. Just because another author finds joy in TikTok doesn't mean you need to.
2. Chasing fame only. If your only measure of success is being famous, burnout comes quickly.
3. Being vague. "I just want people to read my book" is too broad. Specificity leads to strategy.

Friendly Reassurance

Remember: your "why" is yours alone. No one can tell you it's too small or too ambitious. Even if your goal is as modest as selling 100 copies to people you know, that's valid. What matters is aligning your efforts with your vision, so every step feels purposeful rather than pressured.

 **Summary**

- Your "why" is your guiding star in book marketing.
- Defining success on your own terms keeps you focused.
- Readers connect with the purpose behind your writing.
- Your "why" directly shapes your marketing choices.
- A personal mission statement will ground and energize your efforts.

References:

- Brown, B. (2018). *Dare to Lead: Brave Work. Tough Conversations. Whole Hearts.* Random House.
- Sinek, S. (2009). *Start with Why: How Great Leaders Inspire Everyone to Take Action.* Portfolio.
- Thomas, A. (2017). *The Hate U Give.* Balzer + Bray.

CHAPTER 2
UNDERSTANDING YOUR READERS

Imagine you've planned a party. You've cleaned the house, prepared the food, and cued up a great playlist. But when guests arrive, you realize you don't know them—what they like to eat, what music makes them dance, or even why they showed up. That party is probably going to feel a little awkward.

Marketing your book without knowing your readers is like throwing that party. The more clearly you understand who your audience is, the more you can tailor your marketing so it feels like an invitation to something they already want to attend.

Why Audience Matters

Here's a hard truth: your book is not for everyone. And that's a good thing. The publishing world is crowded—millions of titles compete for attention each year. To cut through the noise, you need to speak directly to the people most likely to connect with your work.

Research confirms this: a 2021 Pew Research Center study found that reading habits vary significantly by age, gender, education, and even location (Pew Research Center, 2021). Understanding these patterns helps you find the readers who will resonate with your stories.

General Reading Trends

Here are a few data points to give you context:

1. Women read more than men. In the U.S., 77% of women and 67% of men reported reading at least one book in the past year (Pew, 2021).
2. Age matters. Adults under 30 read more books annually than older groups, but readers 50+ tend to favor nonfiction and history.
3. Format preferences differ. E-book reading is highest among adults under 50, while print remains strong across all ages. Audiobook consumption has nearly doubled in the past decade (Audio Publishers Association, 2022). So when you bring your book to market, consider which formats will make it most successful or if you should release it in as many formats (or even languages as possible, budgeting permitting).
4. Genre loyalty is powerful. Romance, mystery/thriller, and fantasy are perennial top performers. Romance alone accounts for roughly 18% of the U.S. fiction market (NPD Group, 2022).

These patterns don't tell you everything, but they offer clues to where your readers might be and what they might prefer.

Creating a Reader Avatar

A reader avatar is a detailed, fictional profile of your ideal reader. Instead of trying to appeal to "everyone who likes mysteries," you imagine one specific person. This makes your marketing more targeted and personal.

Here's an example:

Name: Sarah Johnson
Age: 42
Occupation: Elementary school teacher
Hobbies: Gardening, true-crime podcasts, weekend book clubs that serve wine
Favorite Coffee Order: Vanilla latte
Why She Reads: To relax after a busy day and escape into small-town stories with lovable characters.

To understand your reader, you may need to do a little online research. For the example above, I looked into who reads cozy mysteries. The answer is overwhelmingly female, over age 40, though younger men, women, and nonbinary people also make up the demographics of cozy mystery readers. The thing in common is that all of these readers prefer character development and problem solving over horror or graphic violence.

When you write a social media post or an email, picture Sarah. Would she find this interesting? Would she feel invited?

EXERCISE:
Build Your Reader Avatar

Grab your notebook and answer these questions: (Google if you have to.)

1. How old is your reader?
2. What's their gender?
3. What do they do for work?
4. What hobbies or passions fill their free time?
5. What formats (print, ebook, audio) do they prefer?
6. Where do they hang out online?
7. Why do they pick up a book like yours?

Don't be afraid to get oddly specific. "She drives a Subaru and always carries an extra tote bag" might sound silly, but specificity makes your marketing voice consistent and relatable.

Why Niche Beats Broad

It's tempting to say, "My book is for everyone who likes good writing." But the most successful authors lean into a niche. Cozy mystery writers thrive because they speak directly to readers who love quirky towns, recurring characters, and crime solved without gore. Science fiction authors often build fandoms by knowing exactly which subgenre their work belongs to—cyberpunk, space opera, dystopian, etc.

Seth Godin calls this finding your "minimum viable audience" (Godin, 2018). Instead of chasing millions of readers, focus on the smaller group that will become loyal fans and spread the word for you.

CASE STUDY:
Brandon Sanderson and the Power of Knowing Your Reader

When it comes to understanding readers, few contemporary authors have built such a strong relationship with their audience as Brandon Sanderson, bestselling fantasy author and professor of creative writing. His career trajectory offers a powerful example of how listening to readers, respecting their expectations, and communicating openly can create a loyal, engaged, and ever-expanding fan base.

The Context: From Aspiring Writer to Fantasy Powerhouse

Sanderson spent years honing his craft before finally breaking into publishing with Elantris in 2005. While he had talent and persistence, his deep success didn't just come from writing good stories—it came from cultivating a two-way relationship with readers. Fantasy is a genre where worldbuilding, series continuity, and fan engagement matter immensely, and Sanderson quickly understood that readers in this space are not passive consumers—they're active participants who crave consistency, detail, and trust.

Strategy 1: Direct Engagement and Radical Transparency

One of Sanderson's most successful practices has been his radical transparency with fans. He maintains an active online presence through his website, newsletters, and social media, where he shares:

Writing Progress Bars: Readers can see exactly how far along he is on current projects (something almost unheard of in publishing). This small visual tool builds trust because readers know he respects their time and anticipation.

Regular Q&A Sessions: He runs AMAs (Ask Me Anything) and livestreams, where he answers detailed reader questions about his books, writing process, and even personal life.

Detailed Release Schedules: Unlike many authors who keep things vague, Sanderson updates fans on timelines and delays openly. Readers respond with patience and loyalty because they feel informed and respected.

Strategy 2: Respecting Reader Expectations Without Being Predictable

Sanderson deeply studies what his readers love about fantasy. Fans of epic fantasy crave:

- Immersive worldbuilding
- Consistent magic systems
- Characters who evolve over time

But he also balances meeting these expectations with surprising twists. For example, his *Mistborn* trilogy begins in a world where the villain has already won—a subversion of traditional fantasy tropes that delighted readers looking for something fresh.

He once explained that he designs his magic systems like puzzles because he knows readers in his genre "love rules and structure." This demonstrates deep knowledge of his audience—not just what they say they want, but what their reading habits show they value.

Strategy 3: The Kickstarter Phenomenon – Trusting the Reader Community

In 2022, Sanderson made headlines when he launched a Kickstarter campaign for four surprise novels he had secretly written during the pandemic. His reasoning: he wanted to give readers direct access to special editions while also experimenting with new publishing models.

The results were staggering:
- The campaign raised $41.7 million from over 185,000 backers—the most successful Kickstarter of all time at that point.
- Readers weren't just buying books; they were investing in Sanderson as a creator. The scale of the campaign showed the depth of loyalty he had built by consistently understanding and respecting his audience.

The success wasn't luck. It came from decades of trust-building: fans knew that if Sanderson promised something, he would deliver it. He had listened to what readers wanted (special editions, direct access, bonus content) and created a model that empowered them.

Strategy 4: Teaching and Empowering Readers

Beyond writing, Sanderson extends his relationship with readers by teaching. He makes his Brigham Young University writing lectures available free on YouTube, reaching aspiring authors worldwide. By doing this, he doesn't just sell books—he creates community and positions himself as both an authority and a mentor.

Readers appreciate this generosity, and it strengthens their loyalty because they see him as someone who genuinely cares about storytelling, not just sales.

The Results: A Loyal Fandom and a Sustainable Business

Sanderson's understanding of his readers has translated into:

- A multimillion-dollar business that includes his own publishing company, Dragonsteel Entertainment.
- A global fanbase who attend conventions, buy special editions, and support him directly through Kickstarter.
- A reputation as one of the most reliable and reader-focused authors in publishing.

His career shows that success isn't just about writing great books—it's about knowing your readers so well that you can anticipate their needs, communicate with them authentically, and create experiences they cherish.

 **Key Takeaways for Authors**

From Sanderson's case study, here are three practical takeaways for any author:

1. **Be Transparent:** Share your process, your challenges, and your wins. Readers appreciate honesty.
2. **Understand What Readers Truly Value:** Go beyond surface-level wants—observe how your readers engage with your genre and what excites them most.
3. **Build Community, Not Just a Sales Base:** Loyal readers aren't just buyers—they're advocates, supporters, and often, collaborators in your success.

Pitfalls to Avoid

1. Assuming you know your readers without research. Just because you like a certain genre doesn't mean your

readers share all your habits.

2. Going too broad. "All adults" is not an audience—it's the whole population.

3. Chasing the wrong trends. If your book isn't a fit for TikTok, forcing it there may feel inauthentic.

 ## Friendly Tip

Remember, defining your readers doesn't mean excluding everyone else. People outside your "avatar" may still love your book. But by aiming your marketing at a clear target, you increase the chances of hitting the bullseye—and the ripple effect brings in others.

 ## Summary

- Your book is not for everyone, and that's good.
- Reading habits differ by demographics, format, and genre.
- A reader avatar makes your marketing voice personal and consistent.
- Niche audiences often generate the strongest loyalty and word of mouth.
- Specificity in knowing your readers leads to smarter, less stressful marketing.

References:

- Pew Research Center. (2021). "Who doesn't read books in America? "Pew Research.
- Audio Publishers Association. (2022). "Audiobook Sales and Consumption Survey."
- NPD Group. (2022). "Romance Market Share in U.S.

Fiction."
- Godin, S. (2018). *This Is Marketing: You Can't Be Seen Until You Learn to See.* Portfolio.

CHAPTER 3
BUILDING YOUR AUTHOR BRAND

When you hear the word "brand", you might think of logos, slogans, and giant corporations like Coca-Cola or Nike. But here's the truth: every author—yes, even you—has a brand. Your brand is simply the story you tell about yourself and the promise you make to your readers.

The good news? You don't need a flashy marketing budget or a design team to create a meaningful author brand. You just need clarity, consistency, and a touch of personality.

What Is an Author Brand?

An author brand is not just your book cover or website. It's the overall impression readers have of you. It includes:

- **Tone:** Are you funny, serious, inspiring, quirky?

- **Values:** What themes consistently show up in your work?
- **Promise:** What do readers know they'll get every time they pick up one of your books?

For example, readers know when they open a Stephen King novel, they'll get suspense and a touch of horror. When they buy a Nora Roberts book, they expect romance with rich emotional arcs. That reliability builds trust.

Why Branding Matters

Branding helps you:

1. **Stand out.** With millions of books available, your unique identity helps readers remember you.
2. **Build loyalty**. A strong brand makes readers come back for your next book.
3. **Simplify decisions.** Branding guides your marketing choices. If your brand is "uplifting and heart-centered," you won't waste time creating snarky, sarcastic content that doesn't fit.

Marketing expert David Aaker describes brand as "a promise to the customer" (Aaker, 1996). For authors, your brand is your promise to your readers.

Elements of an Effective Author Brand

1. **Consistency** – From your website to your Twitter (X) bio, your messaging should align.
2. **Authenticity** – Readers can spot fake personas a mile away.
3. **Clarity** – Keep it simple. Don't try to be everything to everyone.

4. **Emotional Connection**– Brands that stick are the ones that make readers feel something.

Examples of Strong Author Brands

- **James Clear (*Atomic Habits*)** – His brand is clean, practical, and data-driven. His entire online presence reinforces clarity and incremental improvement.
- **Colleen Hoover** – Her brand is raw, emotional romance. She connects authentically with fans on TikTok, making them feel part of her journey.
- **Agatha Christie** – Even decades after her death, her brand is synonymous with clever puzzles and detective intrigue.
- **Jen Sincero** - Her Badass brand is sassy and encouraging and her voice is honest and direct.

 **EXERCISE: Define Your Brand in 50 Words**

Answer these prompts:

1. What themes or topics appear consistently in my work?
2. What do readers say about my writing style?
3. How do I want readers to feel after finishing my book?
4. What three adjectives best describe my writing voice?

Now combine your answers into a 50-word brand statement.

Example from the mystery novelist brother-sister duo who writes as Faith Walker (yes, me and my brother Eric Ferguson):

"We write cozy mysteries set in small-town America, filled with quirky characters, canine sidekicks, and heartwarming humor. Readers can expect a comforting escape, two clever puzzles, and the feeling of belonging to a community. Our brand is about warmth, connection, and a dash of wit."

Visual Branding

Words are the foundation, but visuals matter, too. Consider:

- **Website design:** Colors, fonts, and layout should reflect your tone. A thriller author might use dark, bold colors; a children's author might prefer playful, bright palettes.
- **Headshots:** Professional photos aren't mandatory, but choose images that feel consistent. A smiling, approachable photo works well for rom-coms; a dramatic black-and-white portrait may suit noir mysteries.
- **Book covers:** Readers often judge a book in seconds. Covers should fit your genre while aligning with your personal style. (A pastel watercolor cover would confuse thriller readers!)

Voice and Personality

Your "brand voice" is how you communicate across platforms: social media, newsletters, interviews, even back-cover copy. It should sound like you, only slightly polished.

If you're witty in person, let that shine online. If you're thoughtful and reflective, lean into that. The more your brand matches your authentic self, the easier it is to maintain.

Pitfalls to Avoid

1. **Inconsistency.** If your book is heartfelt but your tweets are sarcastic rants, readers will be confused.
2. **Copying others.** Admiring Colleen Hoover or James Clear is fine, but your brand must reflect you, not a duplicate.
3. **Overcomplicating.** Don't cram every detail of your personality into your brand. Focus on what resonates most with readers.

 CASE STUDY:
Brené Brown

Brené Brown's brand is built around vulnerability, courage, and wholehearted living. Her website, books, talks, and even social media posts all reinforce those themes. Readers trust her because she's consistent, authentic, and clear about her message. That's the essence of powerful branding. (More about Brown's branding in the next chapter)

Mark Manson, author of *The Subtle Art of Not Giving a Fuck,* got a book publishing deal after getting hundreds of thousands of followers to read his website and newsletters. He's a great example of how to build a personal brand. Now let's look at a detailed case study of a nonfiction author who has similarly built a powerful brand that transcends a single book.

 CASE STUDY:
James Clear – Building a Global Brand Around *Atomic Habits*

Background

James Clear is the author of *Atomic Habits* (2018), a book about the science of habit formation and personal improvement. While the book itself became a runaway bestseller (over 20 million copies sold worldwide), what sets Clear apart is the intentional way he built a personal brand—one that feels distinct, trustworthy, and highly valuable. His brand positioning mirrors that of authors like Mark Manson: combining practical, research-backed advice with accessible writing and a clear, consistent voice.

The Brand Identity

Clear's brand is built on three pillars:

1. **Clarity and Simplicity:** His writing distills complex behavioral psychology into actionable, easy-to-understand frameworks. His name itself—"Clear"—has become synonymous with straightforward, no-nonsense advice.
2. **Visual Consistency:** His website, newsletter, and social posts all follow a clean, minimalist aesthetic. This reinforces his brand promise: simplifying the complex.
3. **Trust through Research:** Clear is careful to ground his advice in scientific studies and data, which elevates his authority. Readers perceive him as credible and balanced—not just another self-help guru.

Platform Strategy

Website as a Brand Anchor

Clear's website (jamesclear.com) is a textbook example of how authors can build a brand hub:

- **Homepage Messaging:** "I write about habits, decision-making, and continuous improvement." This tagline immediately defines his niche and audience.
- **Long-Form Articles:** Essays like "The 1% Rule" and "The Four Laws of Behavior Change" give readers free access to the core ideas of his book, encouraging sharing and backlinks.
- **SEO Optimization:** His site ranks highly for keywords around "habits," driving organic traffic long after the book launch.

Newsletter (3-2-1 Thursday)
Perhaps his strongest branding tool, Clear's weekly newsletter has millions of subscribers. The format is consistent:

- 3 short ideas from him
- 2 quotes from others
- 1 question to ponder

This repetition builds familiarity, reinforces his concise writing style, and keeps his brand top-of-mind for readers weekly.

Social Media
Clear uses social media (especially Twitter/X and Instagram) to share bite-sized wisdom, often repurposed from his newsletter or book. His posts are easily shareable, visually consistent, and align with his brand's clarity-first message.

Brand Monetization & Expansion
Clear has kept his brand streamlined, resisting the temptation to expand too quickly into unrelated products. Instead, he's leveraged:

- **Speaking Engagements:** Aligning with corporate clients and leadership organizations.

- **Course Material & Tools:** Supplements that align directly with the Atomic Habits framework.
- **Global Reach:** His book and brand messaging are available in over 50 languages, showing the scalability of a clear, universal brand.

Impact
- *Atomic Habits* has become one of the most influential nonfiction books of the 21st century, often cited alongside classics like *The 7 Habits of Highly Effective People.*
- The 3-2-1 Thursday newsletter has grown into a primary driver of book sales, speaking engagements, and long-term brand awareness.
- Clear is now a thought leader whose name recognition is inseparable from the concept of habits—his core brand promise.

 **Key Takeaways for Authors**

- **Define Your Niche Clearly:** James Clear is "the habits guy." Readers should know exactly what you stand for.
- **Create a Consistent Product:** His newsletter format is predictable but valuable, reinforcing his brand identity with every issue.
- **Leverage Owned Media:** By prioritizing his website and newsletter over platforms he doesn't control, Clear has future-proofed his brand against algorithm changes.
- **Expand Strategically:** Resist the urge to dilute your brand. Everything Clear produces ties back to habits, decision-making, or self-improvement.

Conclusion

James Clear demonstrates that a powerful author brand

isn't built just on one successful book—it's built on clarity, consistency, and the ability to deliver ongoing value to readers. By anchoring his brand in one core idea ("small habits lead to big results"), he has built a trusted, global identity that will outlast the book itself.

EXERCISE:
Create a Brand Mood Board

1. Collect images, colors, and fonts that represent your author personality.
2. Use a tool like Pinterest or Canva to create a digital board or even use an AI image creator like Bing.
3. Include inspirational words or quotes that align with your mission.

This visual guide helps you design consistent marketing materials.

Friendly Tip

Think of your brand not as a rigid box but as a cozy house. It gives structure and comfort, but you can decorate it over time. As you write more books, your brand will evolve—but the foundation will stay the same.

Summary

- Your brand is the story readers tell about you.
- Consistency, authenticity, and clarity make brands memorable.
- Strong author brands promise readers a certain experience every time.
- Define your brand with words, visuals, and voice.

- Keep it authentic—you'll attract the right readers naturally.

References:

- Aaker, D. (1996). *Building Strong Brands*. Free Press.
- Clear, J. (2018). *Atomic Habits*. Avery.
- Brown, B. (2010–2018). Various works on vulnerability and leadership.

CHAPTER 4
GETTING ONLINE WITHOUT GETTING OVERWHELMED

I f the thought of "building an online presence" makes you want to crawl under a blanket, you're not alone. Many authors would rather wrestle with plot holes than figure out websites, mailing lists, or social media algorithms. The good news? You don't need to do everything online to market your book effectively. You just need the right pieces in place.

Think of your online presence like a cozy, welcoming bookstore. You don't need every feature imaginable—you just need a clean front door, a friendly greeter, and a few clear paths that lead people to your book.

Why Online Presence Matters

Even if you plan to sell most of your books in person at events or through word of mouth, readers will still look you up online. A Pew Research Center survey found that 82% of adults in the U.S. read reviews or research online before making purchases, including books (Pew Research Center, 2020). If readers can't find you—or if what they find is confusing—they may move on.

Your online presence does three important things:

1. **Visibility:** It helps new readers discover you.
2. **Credibility:** A professional website and consistent presence make you look like a "real" author.
3. **Connection:** It creates space for readers to engage with you directly.

Author Website Basics

Your website is your online "home base." Unlike social media, it belongs to you. Algorithms change, platforms rise and fall, but your website remains steady.

At minimum, include:

1. Home page: A clear welcome and a quick pitch about who you are and what you write.
2. Books page: Covers, descriptions, and links to buy.
3. About page: A friendly bio with a professional photo.
4. Contact page: A way for readers or the media to reach you.
5. Newsletter signup: Your most important long-term tool (we'll talk about this next).

Keep it simple. You don't need flashing graphics or a dozen pages. A clean, functional site is enough. Tools like WordPress, Wix, GoDaddy, or Squarespace make this manageable even if you're not tech-savvy.

The Magic of Mailing Lists

If you remember only one thing from this chapter, let it be this: your email list is your single most valuable online asset.

Why? Because email is direct. Unlike social media posts that may or may not be shown to followers, emails land right in your readers' inboxes. MarketingSherpa reported that 72% of consumers prefer email as their main channel for brand communication (MarketingSherpa, 2016).

What to send?

- Book updates (new releases, sales, signings).
- Behind-the-scenes notes about your writing process.
- Occasional freebies (bonus stories, printable bookmarks).

Start small. Even if you only have ten subscribers at first, those ten are your most loyal fans.

 **EXERCISE:**

Create a signup form on your website. Offer a "reader magnet"—something free in exchange for an email, like a short story, a sample chapter, or a tip sheet related to your book's theme.

Social Media: Pick Your Spots

Here's where many authors burn out. They try to be everywhere at once—Instagram, Facebook, TikTok, X, LinkedIn, BlueSky, Alignable, Pinterest—and end up exhausted. Don't do that to yourself.

Instead, pick one or two platforms where your readers already hang out. For example:

- **TikTok (BookTok):** Huge for YA, romance, and fantasy.
- **Instagram:** Great for visual genres like cookbooks, children's books, and anything with pretty covers.
- **Facebook:** Still strong for readers 40+, book clubs, and community groups.
- **LinkedIn:** Best for nonfiction, business, and thought leadership.
- **YouTube:** Perfect if you enjoy video and want to build a teaching or storytelling channel.

You don't need to master them all. Choose the one that feels most natural to you and where your target reader avatar (from Chapter 2) spends time.

Content That Works

Don't overthink it. Readers don't expect authors to be influencers. They just want authenticity. Here are content ideas:

- Share progress updates ("I just hit 20,000 words!").
- Post book recommendations (not just your own).
- Share behind-the-scenes peeks of your workspace or pets.
- Ask questions to engage readers.
- Celebrate milestones, big or small.

Remember: engagement matters more than follower counts. Ten readers who feel connected are more valuable than 1,000 who scroll past.

Time-Saving Tools

If the idea of posting regularly feels overwhelming, use scheduling tools like Buffer, Hootsuite, or Later. Set aside an hour once a week to plan posts, then let the software do the posting for you.

Another trick: repurpose content. A blog post can become three social media updates, a newsletter excerpt, and a short video.

 CASE STUDY:
Colleen Hoover – Harnessing Social Media for Explosive Growth

Background

Colleen Hoover is an American author whose career trajectory illustrates the remarkable impact social media can have on an author's visibility and sales. Originally self-published, Hoover's early novels, including *Slammed* (2012), gained traction through word of mouth and enthusiastic readers sharing online. Today, she is one of the best-selling authors in the world, with millions of copies sold, and much of that success can be traced back to her strategic and authentic use of social media.

The Platform: TikTok (#BookTok)

Although Hoover was already a successful author with a

devoted fan base before TikTok became a force, the rise of #BookTok around 2020 amplified her reach exponentially. Readers began posting emotional, candid reactions to her novels—particularly *It Ends with Us* and *Verity*. Videos featuring Hoover's books often went viral, some gaining millions of views. Unlike traditional marketing campaigns, this visibility was organic, created by fans who felt compelled to share their raw reading experiences.

Hoover embraced this momentum rather than trying to control it. She reposted fan content, engaged with readers, and shared behind-the-scenes glimpses of her life and writing. Her presence on TikTok felt approachable and genuine, further fueling fan loyalty.

Strategy in Action

1. **Authenticity First:** Instead of adopting a polished, overly promotional tone, Hoover leaned into her authentic self—quirky, open, and sometimes vulnerable. Readers resonated with her down-to-earth personality as much as her books.
2. **Engagement Over Promotion:** Hoover didn't just post about release dates or sales. She engaged directly with her community—commenting on videos, participating in trends, and celebrating fans' creativity.
3. **User-Generated Content:** Hoover recognized the value of readers' voices. She often amplified user-generated content, which not only validated fans but also created a ripple effect of sharing.
4. **Cross-Platform Integration:** While TikTok was the breakout space, Hoover also leveraged Instagram and Facebook to keep conversations going. She built Facebook groups where readers connected, discussed

her books, and shared recommendations with one another—turning fans into evangelists.

Impact

- By 2021–2022, Hoover dominated bestseller lists. At one point, she had six titles on *The New York Times* list simultaneously.
- Sales of *It Ends with Us*, originally published in 2016, skyrocketed years later due to viral TikTok buzz.
- Hoover's visibility transcended the book world—she was profiled in major outlets like *The New York Times* and *TIME Magazine* and became a household name.

 ## Key Takeaways for Authors

- **Authenticity Wins:** Readers want to connect with the person behind the pen. A genuine voice resonates far more than polished advertising.
- **Empower Your Fans:** Let your readers do the talking. User-generated content is more powerful than any ad campaign.
- **Stay Agile:** Platforms rise and fall. By meeting readers where they were—first on Facebook, then on Instagram, then TikTok—Hoover stayed relevant.
- **Longevity Through Engagement:** Social media doesn't just launch books; it sustains them. Hoover proved that even backlist titles can enjoy new life with the right momentum.

Conclusion

Colleen Hoover's story underscores how social media, when used authentically and interactively, can transform an author's career. For writers navigating today's publishing landscape, her example demonstrates that you don't need a massive ad budget to succeed—what you need is a willingness to connect, engage, and let your readers become your best marketers.

 CASE STUDY:
Brené Brown – Building a Thought Leadership Platform Through Website and Social Media

Background

Brené Brown, a research professor and bestselling author of *Daring Greatly, The Gifts of Imperfection,* and *Atlas of the Heart,* has built an extraordinary career at the intersection of academic research and popular nonfiction. While her ideas about vulnerability, courage, and leadership struck a chord, it was her intentional use of digital platforms—her website, podcasting, and social media—that turned her into a household name.

The Platform Mix

Unlike some authors who rely heavily on one channel, Brown uses an integrated strategy that weaves together her website, email newsletters, podcasts, and multiple social media platforms. Her approach demonstrates how nonfiction authors can create a consistent "ecosystem" of thought leadership, where each platform amplifies and reinforces the others.

Website as a Hub

Brown's website functions as the central hub of her digital presence. It is clean, professional, and user-friendly, providing:

- **Clear Access to Her Books:** Each title has its own landing page with summaries, purchase links, and often companion guides or worksheets.
- **Free Resources:** Brown offers tools, downloads, and blog posts that extend her ideas beyond the page.
- **Podcast Integration:** Her popular shows (*Unlocking Us* and *Dare to Lead*) are directly linked, encouraging cross-pollination between podcast listeners and book readers.
- **Community Connection:** The site includes information on events, courses, and speaking engagements—positioning her not just as an author, but as a movement leader.

Social Media Presence

Brown's social media strategy blends professionalism with approachability:

- **Instagram:** She shares inspiring quotes from her books, personal reflections, and snippets of her life. Visual branding is consistent, using warm tones and text-over-image graphics that are instantly recognizable.
- **Facebook:** She uses longer-form posts, videos, and links to articles or interviews, often sparking deep discussions in the comments.
- **LinkedIn:** Unlike many nonfiction authors, Brown has leaned into LinkedIn, positioning her research within a professional and leadership context. This platform helps her reach organizational leaders and HR professionals who often bring her work into companies.
- **YouTube and Podcasts:** Clips of speaking events and

podcast episodes create accessible entry points for new audiences.

Strategy in Action

1. **Multi-Channel Cohesion:** Every platform connects back to her core themes—vulnerability, courage, shame resilience—creating brand clarity.
2. **Generosity of Content:** She shares a significant amount of material for free (quotes, clips, exercises), which builds trust and positions her as a thought leader rather than a salesperson.
3. **Storytelling with Authenticity:** Even on professional platforms like LinkedIn, Brown shows vulnerability, embodying the very principles she writes about.
4. **Cross-Promotion:** Podcasts drive traffic to books, books lead to speaking engagements, and her website ties it all together.

Impact

- Brown's TED Talk ("The Power of Vulnerability") became one of the most watched in the world, largely because her website and social channels made it easy to find, share, and connect with her other work.
- Her books have sold millions of copies worldwide, consistently landing on bestseller lists.
- She built not just an audience, but a community of readers and leaders who integrate her work into schools, workplaces, and organizations.

 **Key Takeaways for Nonfiction Authors**

- **Your Website Is Home Base:** Social media platforms

change, but your website is the one space you fully own. Make it professional, resource-rich, and aligned with your brand.

- **Be a Thought Leader, Not Just an Author:** Share ideas, frameworks, and stories that position you as an authority in your field.
- **Different Platforms, Different Audiences:** Use Instagram for inspiration, LinkedIn for professionals, Facebook for community, etc.
- **Authenticity + Consistency = Trust:** Brown's readers trust her because her brand, voice, and messaging are consistent across every channel.

Conclusion

Brené Brown demonstrates that nonfiction authors can leverage websites and social media to move beyond book sales and build lasting influence. By treating her digital presence as an ecosystem of ideas rather than a promotional tool, she has expanded her reach, built a devoted global following, and created cultural conversations that extend far beyond her books.

Pitfalls to Avoid

1. Trying to do it all. Spreading yourself too thin means doing nothing well.
2. Inconsistent presence. Posting daily for a week then vanishing for months confuses readers.
3. Focusing only on selling. Constant "buy my book" posts feel pushy. Balance sales with authentic connection.

 **EXERCISE:**
Online Presence Checklist

1. Do I have a clean, simple website with a way to buy my book?
2. Do I have a mailing list signup on my site?
3. Have I chosen one or two social platforms that fit my readers?
4. Do I have a plan to post or send updates at least once or twice a month?

If you can answer "yes" to all four, you're set.

 Friendly Reassurance

You don't need to become a social media star. Your goal is not to compete with influencers—it's to create a discoverable, welcoming online space for your readers. Start small, keep it manageable, and build from there.

 **Summary**

- An online presence is your author storefront.
- A simple website and mailing list are essential.
- Social media is optional—pick the platforms that fit your readers and your personality.
- Engagement beats follower counts every time.
- Small, consistent steps prevent overwhelm.

References:

- Pew Research Center. (2020). "Online Shopping and E-commerce."
- MarketingSherpa. (2016). "Customer Communication Preferences Survey."

CHAPTER 5
SOCIAL MEDIA WITH SANITY

For authors, social media can feel like both a blessing and a curse. On one hand, it offers a direct line to readers and the potential for viral success. On the other, it can be overwhelming, time-consuming, and, at times, discouraging. This chapter is about keeping the benefits while minimizing the stress.

Why Social Media Matters (in Moderation)

Social media is not optional for many authors, but it doesn't need to dominate your life. A 2023 Statista survey showed that 59% of U.S. adults use at least one social platform daily (Statista, 2023). That means readers are already there, scrolling, discovering, and talking about books.

The key word? Moderation. Social media should support your writing life, not replace it. So, how can we do this, so that you don't go to post and end up losing two hours watching cat videos?

Set Clear Goals

Before posting, ask yourself: What do I want social media to do for me? Common goals include:

1. **Building awareness:** Helping new readers discover your work.
2. **Nurturing community:** Deepening connections with existing readers.
3. **Driving sales:** Encouraging people to buy your book (best achieved through subtlety).
4. **Networking:** Connecting with fellow authors, bloggers, and reviewers.

Pick two of these to focus on. Trying to hit all four at once is where burnout begins...and trying to hit all four is an excellent way to muddle your message.

Choosing the Right Platform

Every platform has a personality. Instead of chasing trends, find the one that fits your voice and audience:

- **Facebook:** Excellent for older demographics, book clubs, and event promotion.
- **Instagram:** Visual, great for cover reveals, quotes, and "aesthetic" content.
- **TikTok:** The powerhouse for BookTok. Particularly strong in romance, fantasy, and YA.

- **X (formerly Twitter):** Ideal for networking with writers, agents, and journalists, though less reliable for direct book sales.
- **LinkedIn:** Best for nonfiction, business, or professional expertise.
- **Pinterest:** Useful for lifestyle or hobby-based nonfiction (cookbooks, crafts, DIY).

 **EXERCISE:**

Write down your target reader avatar (from Chapter 2). Where do they spend time online? Start there and ignore the rest.

The 80/20 Rule

A healthy balance on social media is about 80% engagement and value and 20% promotion.

- Engagement (80%): Share behind-the-scenes moments, inspirational quotes, pet photos, questions, or content related to your genre.
- Promotion (20%): Announce sales, signings, or new releases.

And taking this even further, the course on social media marketing by Strong Brand Social, recommends making the majority of that engagement part of your content about your avatar. (Think of the way REI and Patagonia show people doing outdoor things on their social media channels; they don't say, "Hey, buy our products." They show situations their ideal customers can relate to and things they love.) The ratio they recommend is 60% about your reader, 20% about you, and 15–20% can be promotional.

This balance keeps your feed interesting while still moving books. (And it doesn't make you look like your feed is all about you.) :)

Creating Content Without Losing Your Mind

Social media shouldn't feel like a full-time job. Here are manageable content types:

1. **Behind-the-scenes:** A photo of your writing desk or coffee mug.
2. **Quotes:** Lines from your book or favorite authors.
3. **Reader spotlights:** Share photos of readers with your book.
4. **Short videos:** A 30-second clip explaining your writing routine or answering a reader question. Or you could even do a video on potential cover designs and have your readers vote the one that gets used.
5. **Themed posts:** #ThrowbackThursday (share an early draft), #FridayReads (recommend a book).

Tip: Reuse content. A blog post can be broken into short quotes for Instagram, a reel for TikTok, and a discussion question for Facebook.

Scheduling for Sanity

You don't need to be "always online." Tools like Buffer, Later, and Hootsuite allow you to batch posts once a week.

A simple schedule:

- 1–2 posts per week on your main platform.
- 1 story or reel if you enjoy creating and editing video.

- Reply to comments/messages within a day or two.

That's it. Consistency beats volume.

 ## CASE STUDY:
V.E. Schwab – Building a Loyal Fandom Through Social Media Storytelling

Background

Victoria "V.E." Schwab is the bestselling fantasy author of *The Invisible Life of Addie LaRue*, the *Shades of Magic* trilogy, and numerous other novels for adults, teens, and children. What makes Schwab an excellent case study is not just her sales success, but the way she has cultivated a deeply engaged community online by merging her fictional storytelling with personal transparency.

The Platforms

Schwab has been highly active across Instagram, TikTok, and Twitter/X, each serving a slightly different function in her brand ecosystem:

- **Instagram:** Behind-the-scenes looks at her creative process, photos of her travels, and personal reflections.
- **TikTok:** Fan-centered content, humorous takes on the writing life, and promotional but playful book-related videos.
- **Twitter/X:** Real-time engagement with fans, writing updates, and conversations about industry challenges.

Strategy in Action

1. Personal Vulnerability + Author Transparency

Schwab has been open about her struggles with anxiety, the realities of the publishing industry, and the challenges of sustaining creativity. This candidness has made her relatable to fans and aspiring writers alike. Rather than positioning herself as a "distant" author, she presents herself as a fellow traveler on the creative journey.

2. Fandom Engagement

Schwab treats her fandom not as passive readers, but as a community. She shares fan art, responds to reader posts, and occasionally teases upcoming projects. By acknowledging and amplifying fan contributions, she strengthens their emotional investment in her stories.

3. Storytelling Beyond the Page

Schwab's posts often mirror the themes of her books: identity, longing, resilience, and belonging. She uses quotes from her works, aesthetic photos, and tone-setting captions that feel like extensions of her novels. This creates a seamless brand identity—her social media is not separate from her fiction, but an echo of it.

4. Consistency and Voice

Even as platforms shift, Schwab has maintained a consistent online persona: thoughtful, slightly whimsical, candid, and empowering. Readers know what to expect from her voice whether they are on Instagram, TikTok, or reading her newsletter.

Impact

- *The Invisible Life of Addie LaRue* became a cultural phenomenon in part due to social media buzz, with readers sharing emotional reactions, annotated pages, and elaborate fan art. Schwab amplified this momentum by reposting and engaging, which created a feedback loop of visibility.

- Schwab's Instagram following (hundreds of thousands strong) provides a built-in audience for each new release, while TikTok gives her access to younger readers discovering her backlist for the first time.

- By positioning herself as both a storyteller and a human with struggles and triumphs, she has fostered unusually strong reader loyalty. Many of her fans buy multiple editions of the same book (special editions, foreign editions, signed copies)—a testament to the brand identity she has built.

 ## Key Takeaways for Authors

1. **Let Your Brand Reflect Your Fiction:** Schwab's social presence feels like an extension of her books' themes, creating continuity between her art and her persona.

2. **Show Up Authentically:** Transparency about the ups and downs of writing builds trust and relatability.

3. **Celebrate Your Readers:** Amplifying fan art, reviews, and reactions not only validates readers but also creates more incentive for others to share.

4. **Stay Consistent Across Platforms:** Even while tailoring posts to each channel, maintain a recognizable voice and aesthetic.

Conclusion

V.E. Schwab exemplifies how fiction authors can use social media not just to promote books, but to create worlds that live beyond the page. By blending personal authenticity with community engagement and thematic storytelling, Schwab has built a brand that ensures readers will follow her from one book—or even one genre—to the next.

Handling Negativity

One downside of social media is criticism. Trolls happen. Here are strategies for dealing with haters:

1. Pause before responding. Most negativity doesn't deserve your energy.
2. Use the block/mute button freely. Protect your mental space.
3. Engage thoughtfully with constructive criticism. If a reader offers genuine feedback, thank them.

Remember: your goal is to connect with readers who enjoy your work, not to convince everyone.

Here's a concise but detailed case study on how a well-known author turned social media negativity into an opportunity for connection:

 CASE STUDY:
Neil Gaiman – Responding to Negativity with Wit and Grace

Background

Neil Gaiman, author of *American Gods, Coraline,* and *The Sandman,* is not only celebrated for his fiction but also for his approachable and thoughtful presence online. With millions of followers on Twitter/X and Tumblr, Gaiman has often faced criticism, trolling, or negativity. Instead of retreating, he has built his brand partly on the way he responds—with wit, kindness, and a touch of storytelling.

The Situation

Over the years, Gaiman has received negative comments ranging from dismissive takes on his writing to outright trolling. One well-circulated example involved a reader who complained that his book *The Ocean at the End of the Lane* "wasn't worth the money." Rather than ignoring the remark or lashing out, Gaiman replied calmly, reminding the critic (and everyone watching) that not every book is for every reader— and that it's okay.

The Response

- **Calm and Respectful:** Gaiman rarely takes offense. Instead, he acknowledges the person's opinion without escalating.
- **Humor as Deflection:** When trolls attack in bad faith, he often uses dry humor to neutralize hostility and entertain his wider audience.
- **Empathy and Perspective:** He sometimes reframes negativity as an opportunity to remind readers of the subjectivity of art, or to share encouragement for other authors who might be watching.

Impact

- **Community Trust:** By handling negativity gracefully, Gaiman reinforces his image as approachable, wise, and unflappable.
- **Audience Amplification:** His clever, kind responses

often go viral, generating more goodwill than the original criticism could have damaged.

- **Longevity:** Instead of being drawn into endless online fights, his strategy protects his energy while modeling how authors can engage with critics without alienating fans.

 ## Key Takeaways for Authors

1. **Don't Engage in Battles:** Fighting negativity only amplifies it.
2. **Use Humor Wisely:** A touch of wit can deflate hostility without seeming defensive.
3. **Acknowledge Subjectivity:** Remind audiences that not every book will work for every reader—and that's okay.
4. **Think About the Silent Audience:** Most people watch interactions without commenting; graceful handling of negativity strengthens your broader reputation.

Conclusion

Neil Gaiman shows that authors don't need to fear social media negativity. By approaching critics with respect, humor, and perspective, he transforms potential conflict into brand-building moments of connection—proving that how you respond can matter more than what was said in the first place.

Let's look at one more case study dealing with turning negativity into something better, this time with a nonfiction author.

 ## CASE STUDY:
Roxane Gay – Turning Negativity Into Dialogue and Boundaries

Background

Roxane Gay, acclaimed author of *Bad Feminist, Hunger,* and *Difficult Women,* is known not only for her incisive essays and fiction but also for her bold, unfiltered presence on social media. With hundreds of thousands of followers across platforms, she often engages directly with conversations about feminism, race, body image, and culture. These topics, while central to her work, also attract trolls and critics.

The Situation

Gay frequently faces negativity online—ranging from dismissive remarks about her feminism, to body shaming, to harassment from political or cultural detractors. Instead of retreating from public discourse, she has developed a distinctive style of handling negativity that aligns with her brand as a sharp, no-nonsense cultural critic.

The Response

- **Directness and Clarity:** Gay does not sugarcoat. She often responds directly to negativity with a clear, pointed rebuttal. For example, when attacked with body-shaming comments, she has matter-of-factly reminded critics that their attempts to shame her do not erase her humanity or success.
- **Setting Boundaries:** Gay has spoken openly about blocking people liberally. She views blocking as self-care, not censorship. This sends a clear message: she

controls her digital space.

- **Using Negativity as Content:** At times, Gay highlights absurd or hateful comments to demonstrate larger cultural problems, reframing personal attacks as teachable moments for her audience.
- **Humor and Sharp Wit:** She often responds with humor that undercuts cruelty. Her wit allows her to flip the narrative, leaving the critic diminished and her supporters uplifted.

Impact

- **Community Strength:** By confronting negativity head-on, Gay models for her readers—particularly women, LGBTQ+ people, and marginalized communities—that it's valid to set boundaries and stand firm online.
- **Personal Brand:** Her responses reinforce her brand identity: unapologetically outspoken, sharp, and unwilling to be diminished.
- **Empowerment of Audience:** Many fans find strength in her example, citing her willingness to speak back to harassment as both brave and necessary.

 ## Key Takeaways for Authors

1. **Own Your Space:** You don't have to tolerate harassment—blocking and muting are legitimate tools.
2. **Reframe Negativity:** Use hostile comments as opportunities to highlight cultural issues or spark dialogue.
3. **Stay True to Your Voice:** Gay's unapologetic style works because it aligns with her writing and public persona. The key is consistency.
4. **Model Boundaries for Your Audience:** Many readers

look to authors as role models for handling criticism—your response can inspire others.

Conclusion

Roxane Gay exemplifies a strategy for authors facing hostility on social media: respond directly when it matters, block when necessary, and never allow negativity to silence your voice. By treating her platforms as extensions of her authorship—spaces for sharp critique, humor, and boundary-setting—she has transformed negativity into both empowerment and brand strength.

Protecting Your Writing Time

Social media should not steal your writing hours. (And I get how difficult that can be at times. I get sucked into watching videos and reddit feeds of red heeler cattle dog puppies, so I feel you.) Try these habits:

- Set a timer for 15 minutes when checking feeds.
- Move apps off your home screen to reduce impulse scrolling.
- Decide your "posting days" and stick to them.

Your book is your greatest marketing tool. Don't sacrifice it for endless posting, especially with content you've created to create content. Save the posting for when you have something to say.

 **QUICK CHECKLIST:**
Social Media with Sanity

1. Do I know my top two goals for social media?

2. Have I chosen the platform that fits my readers best?
3. Am I following the 80/20 rule?
4. Do I have a posting schedule that feels sustainable?
5. Am I protecting my writing time from endless scrolling?

If you can say "yes" to all five, you're using social media with sanity.

 **Summary**

- Social media works best when it has clear goals.
- Choose platforms based on your audience, not popularity.
- Balance content: mostly engagement, some promotion.
- Consistency is better than constant posting.
- Protect your mental health and your writing time.

References:

- Statista. (2023). "Share of U.S. Adults Using Social Media Daily."
- MarketingSherpa. (2016). "Customer Communication Preferences Survey."

CHAPTER 6
REVIEWS, WORD OF MOUTH, ENDORSEMENTS, AND STREET TEAMS

When a reader is deciding whether to buy your book, they usually don't just look at the cover or the blurb—they look for social proof. Reviews, blurbs, and endorsements tell them, "This book is worth your time." In fact, surveys show that 79% of people trust online reviews as much as personal recommendations (BrightLocal, 2020). For authors, this makes reviews and endorsements essential.

In this chapter, we'll explore how to gather them ethically, use them strategically, and even harness a community of readers— your "street team"—to help spread the word.

Why Reviews Matter

Reviews influence both algorithms and readers. Here's how:

1. **Algorithms:** Amazon, Goodreads, and other platforms use review activity as a signal. More reviews often mean more visibility in recommendations and searches.
2. **Reader trust:** A book with zero reviews looks risky. A book with 50+ reviews, even if they're a mix of positive and critical, appears credible.
3. **Social proof:** Reviews help readers imagine what kind of experience they'll have.

A 2019 Nielsen Book Research study found that readers who see 10 or more reviews are more than twice as likely to purchase compared to those who see fewer (Nielsen, 2019).

Gathering Reviews Ethically

(And yes, I said ethically because services overseas are happy to promise you dozens or hundreds or thousands of reviews for a certain price tag. Review mills are a thing.)

It's tempting to ask family and friends for glowing reviews, but Amazon has strict guidelines against "biased reviews." Violating them can get reviews deleted—or even accounts suspended.

Instead, try these strategies:

1. **Advance Reader Copies (ARCs):** Send free digital or print copies to readers in exchange for an honest review. Services like NetGalley or BookSirens can help.
2. **Book bloggers and reviewers:** Reach out to bloggers

who cover your genre. Many post review policies on their sites.

3. **Goodreads giveaways:** Offer copies in exchange for reviews.
4. **Beta readers:** Early readers can double as reviewers once your book launches.
5. **Call-to-action in your book:** At the end, include a friendly note asking readers to leave a review if they enjoyed it.

Crafting a Review Request

Readers are more likely to review if you make it easy. A simple message works best:

Sample Email:

"Hi, [Name],
Thank you so much for reading [Book Title]! If you enjoyed it, would you consider leaving an honest review on Amazon or Goodreads? Reviews help readers discover new books and mean so much to independent authors like me.
Here's the link: [Insert link]
With gratitude,
[Your Name]"

Notice the emphasis on honest—this reassures readers that you're not fishing for only positive feedback.

Endorsements and Blurbs

Endorsements (or blurbs) are those short praise quotes you see on book covers or inside front pages. They carry weight because they come from established voices—authors, experts, or notable figures in your field.

How to Get Them:

1. **Start with your network:** Do you know anyone respected in your genre? Ask.
2. **Reach out respectfully:** Email authors or experts with a concise request. Attach a summary, not the full manuscript unless they agree.
3. **Make it easy:** Suggest they provide just one or two sentences.
4. **Give plenty of time:** Two to three months before your publication date is best.

Sample Outreach:

"Dear [Name],
I admire your work in [genre/topic] and think readers of my upcoming book, [Title], would connect with your perspective. Would you be open to reading an advance copy and, if it resonates, offering a short endorsement? I'd be honored to feature your words on the cover or in the opening pages.
Thank you for considering,
[Your Name]"

Endorsements aren't just decoration—they can also sway bookstores and media outlets when you pitch your book.

Tip: One thing you should note is that some people who agree to write an endorsement for your book may ask for a few samples or what you'd like the endorsement to say. It is okay to provide a draft endorsement or two or a few that they can choose from and then modify as they see fit. The reality is that some people endorse books without actually reading the whole book. I know this may be a shock, but it is true.

But do not provide samples until you are asked for them by the endorser.

And always, always send a thank-you note to the person who endorsed your book, and when your book is published, send them a signed copy as a thank-you gift. That's the classy thing to do.

Building a Street Team or a Launch Team

A street team is a group of enthusiastic supporters who help promote your book. Think of them as your cheerleaders and word-of-mouth champions.

Who They Are:
- Loyal readers.
- Friends who genuinely enjoy your work.
- Bookstagrammers, TikTok reviewers, or book club members.

What They Do:
- Post reviews on launch day.
- Share your book on social media.
- Hand out bookmarks or flyers at local events.
- Invite others to your signings or online launches.

How to Build A Street Team or Launch Team:
1. **Recruit early:** Ask in your newsletter, on social media, during any public speaking events you do, or in your reader groups.
2. **Give perks:** Free copies, exclusive Q&A sessions, behind-the-scenes updates.

3. **Keep them engaged:** Share milestones, sneak peeks, and personal thank-yous.
4. **Celebrate them:** Publicly thank your team in your acknowledgments or on social media.

A street team doesn't need to be huge—even 20 dedicated supporters can make a visible impact on launch week.

 CASE STUDY:
How Jennifer L. Armentrout Built a Powerhouse Street Team to Launch Her Books

One of the most successful examples of leveraging a street team in the fiction world is Jennifer L. Armentrout, a bestselling author of YA (young adult), NA (new adult), and romance. Her "street team" approach helped catapult her books onto bestseller lists, build a thriving fandom, and sustain long-term sales momentum.

The Situation: A Growing Author with Wide Appeal

By the early 2010s, Jennifer L. Armentrout had already released several successful books, but she was competing in highly saturated genres—paranormal romance, fantasy, and new adult. While her books were gaining traction, she needed a way to:

- Generate buzz before release dates
- Reach new readers outside her existing fan base
- Encourage sustained word-of-mouth marketing

She recognized that her most passionate readers were not just consumers—they could be ambassadors.

The Strategy: Building the "Jenuine Armentrout Street Team"

Armentrout created an official street team for her books, giving them a unique name and branding by playing on her first name and the word genuine. She treated membership as both a privilege and a community, offering exclusive perks while asking members to actively support her launches.

Key elements of her strategy included:

1. Selective Recruitment
- Readers applied for a spot by demonstrating enthusiasm and past support for her books.
- This ensured only truly engaged fans joined, keeping the group highly motivated.

2. Exclusive Perks
- Early access to ARCs (advance review copies).
- Private Facebook group for team members to connect.
- Exclusive Q&As with the author.
- Swag and giveaways only for the team.

3. Clear Calls-to-Action
Members were asked to:

- Post honest reviews on Amazon, Goodreads, and blogs.
- Share book news on social media.
- Organize local book club reads or library requests.
- Participate in launch countdowns and themed posts.

4. Gamification
- Armentrout turned promotion into a friendly

competition.

- Members earned points for tasks (e.g., sharing posts, posting reviews, creating fan art).
- Top contributors won signed books, swag, or even video chats with the author.

The Execution: How It Worked in Practice

One notable example was the launch of her *Lux* series continuation and later her *Blood and Ash* books. In the months leading up to release:

- Street team members created a steady drumbeat of excitement across Twitter, Instagram, and Goodreads.
- Fans posted teaser graphics, countdown memes, and shared personal excitement.
- On release week, reviews flooded in within the first 24–48 hours, boosting visibility on Amazon's algorithms.
- The private Facebook group gave team members a sense of ownership—they weren't just readers, they were part of the author's inner circle.

Armentrout herself remained highly visible and approachable, frequently interacting with her team, sharing behind-the-scenes peeks into her writing process, and publicly thanking them for their support. This created loyalty that went beyond a single book launch.

Results

The street team approach produced measurable outcomes:

- **Explosive Early Reviews:** Hundreds of reviews appeared on Amazon and Goodreads within days of launch, driving discoverability.

- **Chart Placement:** Several of her books, including From Blood and Ash, hit bestseller lists largely because of the coordinated early push.
- **Sustained Engagement:** Fans kept promoting her books long after launch, especially through word-of-mouth and book clubs.
- **Fandom Culture:** Her team helped grow a thriving online community that expanded into fan art, TikTok edits, and consistent buzz every time she announced a new project.

Why It Worked

1. **Reciprocity** – By giving fans exclusive content and access, she created loyalty.
2. **Community** – Fans didn't just join for her; they bonded with each other.
3. **Empowerment** – Team members felt like they were contributing to her success in a meaningful way.
4. **Consistency** – She maintained her team across multiple launches, compounding its effect over time.

 ## Key Takeaways for Authors

- **Start Small, Grow Big:** You don't need hundreds of people. Even 15–30 dedicated readers can make a noticeable impact.
- **Offer Real Value:** ARCs, swag, or just private Q&A time with you can be enough.
- **Make It Fun:** Turn participation into games, challenges, or countdowns.
- **Be Accessible:** The more approachable you are, the more loyal your team will remain.

- **Reward and Recognize:** A personal thank-you goes a long way toward keeping motivation high.

Conclusion

Jennifer L. Armentrout's success with street teams illustrates how authors can transform readers into active promoters. By treating her fans as collaborators rather than passive consumers, she not only launched books successfully but also built a sustained ecosystem of excitement around her entire career.

Her model shows that when done well, a launch team is not just a short-term tactic—it's a long-term investment in community and word-of-mouth marketing.

Nonfiction authors often face a different challenge than novelists: their books compete not only with other authors but also with podcasts, newsletters, and YouTube channels in the crowded "ideas" marketplace. To stand out, many nonfiction writers turn to launch teams to create early momentum and credibility.

One of the best examples is Gretchen Rubin, bestselling author of *The Happiness Project* and *Better Than Before*. Rubin used a carefully cultivated launch team and early reader community to expand her reach from a niche blog into an international bestselling brand.

 CASE STUDY:
How Gretchen Rubin Leveraged a Launch Team to Spread *The Happiness Project*

The Situation: From Blog to Bookstore

Before her breakout book, Rubin was already building an audience through her blog on happiness and habits. She had an engaged readership, but when *The Happiness Project* was preparing for launch in 2009, she knew she needed more than traditional publicity. She needed a way to:

- Mobilize her loyal online followers to spread the word.
- Seed early reviews and testimonials.
- Build grassroots enthusiasm that felt authentic rather than corporate.

The Strategy: Recruiting "Super Fans" into a Happiness Project Launch Team

Rubin reached out to her most active blog readers and newsletter subscribers to form what she called her "Street Team for Happiness."

Core features of her launch team strategy:
1. **Exclusive Previews**
   - Members got sneak peeks at book chapters and early access to bonus content.
   - This gave them a sense of insider status—like they were seeing the book before the rest of the world.
2. **Personalized Involvement**
   - Rubin encouraged members to share their own happiness experiments and results, making them feel like co-creators in the movement.
   - She featured some of these stories on her blog and in her newsletter, giving recognition that motivated deeper participation.
3. **Amplification Through Authentic Channels**
   - Launch team members were encouraged to talk

about the book on their personal blogs, Facebook (then just gaining traction as a book marketing tool), and Goodreads.

- Instead of copy-pasting press blurbs, Rubin suggested they share personal takeaways—a tactic that made their endorsements feel organic.

4. **Early Review Seeding**
   - The team helped flood Amazon and Goodreads with early reviews, giving the book immediate social proof.

5. **Community Identity**
   - Members felt like part of a movement larger than a single book—"The Happiness Project" wasn't just Gretchen's project, it became their project too.

The Execution: Launching *The Happiness Project*

Rubin's launch team became a visible force:

- Bloggers and influencers (before the word "influencer" was widespread) wrote posts about their own happiness projects, linking back to Rubin's book.
- Dozens of early readers left authentic Amazon reviews within the first week, pushing the book higher in rankings.
- The book gained traction with word-of-mouth through book clubs and workplaces, where launch team members introduced it as a group read.

Rubin herself remained present—replying to emails, commenting on blog posts, and featuring her readers' stories— which deepened loyalty.

Results

- *The Happiness Project* debuted on *The New York Times* bestseller list and stayed there for more than two years.
- Early buzz helped secure international translations and a wide readership far beyond Rubin's initial blog audience.
- Her street team became the seed for what later grew into her Habits and Happiness community, which continues through her podcasts, newsletters, and workshops.
- Word-of-mouth propelled not only the launch but also long-term sales—a key distinction of her approach.

Why It Worked

1. **Personal Connection:** Readers felt like Rubin genuinely cared about their happiness journeys.
2. **Community-Building:** She created a movement rather than a one-off book.
3. **Early Social Proof:** Dozens of reviews and testimonials signaled credibility to new readers.
4. **Sustained Engagement:** By continuing to interact with her launch team beyond the book's debut, she kept enthusiasm alive for years.

 ## Key Takeaways for Authors

- **Tap Your Core Readers:** Even a blog audience of a few hundred can become a powerful launch team if mobilized.
- **Make It Personal:** Encourage launch team members to share their own stories and connect your book's theme to their lives.

- **Recognition is Gold:** Highlighting a launch team member's contribution (a testimonial, blog post, or review) creates immense goodwill.
- **Think Beyond the Launch:** Build a long-term community around your topic, not just a one-off event.

Conclusion

Gretchen Rubin's use of a launch team demonstrates how nonfiction authors can turn a book into a movement. By giving readers ownership, recognition, and an active role in spreading her message, she transformed her audience into loyal advocates.

Her approach underscores that a launch team is not just about moving copies—it's about creating lasting cultural resonance for the ideas inside the book.

Common Pitfalls to Avoid

1. **Buying fake reviews:** Amazon cracks down on this. Readers can spot them instantly.
2. **Pressuring readers for positive reviews:** Always ask for honesty, not five stars.
3. **Neglecting to follow up:** Sometimes people forget. A gentle reminder is fine.
4. **Ignoring your reviewers:** Thank them. A quick reply goes a long way.

 QUICK CHECKLIST:
Reviews, Endorsements, Street Teams

1. Have I created a plan to gather reviews ethically?

2. Do I know who I'll approach for endorsements?
3. Have I drafted a polite, concise review request email?
4. Am I building a small but engaged street team?
5. Do I avoid shortcuts like buying reviews?

 ## Summary

- Reviews matter because they drive algorithms and reader trust.
- Gather reviews through ARCs, bloggers, and polite requests.
- Endorsements add authority and credibility.
- A street or launch team creates word-of-mouth momentum.
- Authenticity and gratitude keep your supporters invested.

References:

- BrightLocal. (2020). "Local Consumer Review Survey."
- Nielsen Book Research. (2019). "Understanding the Book Buyer."

CHAPTER 7
LAUNCH WEEK LIKE A PRO

After months (or years) of writing, revising, and preparing, your book is finally ready to meet the world. Launch week is your moment in the spotlight. But here's the truth: the best launches don't happen by accident. They are carefully orchestrated campaigns designed to maximize visibility, excitement, and sales within a short, high-energy window.

Think of launch week as both a celebration and a strategy. This is when all your marketing efforts—social media, email lists, endorsements, street teams—come together to create momentum.

Why Launch Week Matters

Book sales often follow a "burst and fade" pattern. A strong first week can:

1. **Boost visibility:** Many platforms, including Amazon, rank books based on early sales velocity. A surge in purchases puts you in "Customers Also Bought" sections.
2. **Attract media attention:** Journalists and bloggers are more likely to cover a book that's creating buzz.
3. **Build long-term momentum:** A launch can set the tone for months of sales. Even if you don't hit bestseller lists, concentrated activity can make your book discoverable far beyond launch week.

According to Bowker (2020), books with planned launch campaigns sold, on average, "40% more copies in their first three months" than those without coordinated efforts.

Pre-Launch Checklist (2–3 Months Before)

Success during launch week comes from groundwork laid earlier. By the time your book is published, you want your audience to be primed and excited.

1. **Finalize your book:** Proof, format, and upload your files so technical issues don't derail your launch.
2. **Set a firm release date:** This gives your team something to rally around.
3. **Build anticipation:** Share cover reveals, sneak peeks, and countdowns.
4. **Line up reviewers and endorsements:** Make sure ARCs are already out in the world. And then start collecting

the endorsements that will go on the book's cover and interior, on your Amazon Author page and maybe in the description of the book on the bookstore websites, and on social media.

5. Whether or not you are working with a publicist, **start lining up media interviews** by sending podcast hosts and producers, print media, and bloggers ARCs of your book, along with a press kit that contains a press release, a headshot, and a list of questions with your answers (so that interviewers can use those are a starting point).

6. **Prepare launch assets:** Graphics, teasers, video trailers, and additional press releases to specific audiences.

7. **Coordinate with your street or launch team:** Give them instructions on how to post, when to review, and where to share.

Crafting a Launch Week Schedule

A good launch isn't about spamming your audience—it's about creating a rhythm of excitement. Here's a sample day-by-day structure for your launch week:

Day 1: Launch Announcement
- Send a celebratory newsletter.
- Post on all social channels.
- Thank your early supporters.
- Encourage readers to share photos of the book with a unique hashtag.

Day 2: Social Proof Spotlight
- Share early reviews, endorsements, or blurbs.
- Post testimonials on Instagram or Twitter with eye-catching graphics.

Day 3: Behind-the-Scenes Day
- Share your writing journey, challenges, and fun facts.
- Post a short video of you reading a favorite passage.

Day 4: Giveaway or Contest
- Host a giveaway (signed copy, swag, gift cards).
- Ask participants to share your book or leave reviews to enter.

Day 5: Media Push
- Publish guest blogs, podcast interviews, or local media features.
- Post clips and links to these appearances.

Day 6: Reader Engagement
- Host a Q&A on Facebook Live, Instagram, or YouTube.
- Share reader photos or posts (with permission).

Day 7: Gratitude and Momentum
- Post a heartfelt thank-you to readers, reviewers, and your team.
- Invite readers to tell friends or post their reviews.
- Announce what's next (e.g., your next book project or a book club discussion).

Leveraging Your Street Team

Your street team becomes especially powerful during launch week. Encourage them to:

- Post reviews on Amazon, Barnes and Noble, Goodreads, and BookBub the day of launch. (They can copy and paste the same review to all sites.)
- Share graphics, teasers, and quotes on their personal

networks.
- Join your online events to boost participation.

Make it fun—create challenges like "Who can post the most creative book photo?" and reward them with swag or exclusive access.

Social Media Strategies

Not all social platforms are equal for every genre. Consider your audience:

- Instagram & TikTok: Great for YA, romance, fantasy, lifestyle nonfiction. Use reels, book aesthetic photos, and reader challenges.
- Facebook: Strong for nonfiction, memoirs, and genres targeting older readers. Use events, groups, and live streams.
- Twitter (X): Good for professional nonfiction, sci-fi, and speculative fiction. Use threads, quotes, and hashtags.
- LinkedIn: Best for business or self-help. Post thought leadership content tied to your book.

Tip: Don't just say, "Buy my book." Share stories, quotes, or visuals that invite people in. And make sure if you are doing book signings or author events that these get posted to your preferred social media channels, your website, added to your newsletters, etc.

Traditional and Local Media

While much of marketing is online, don't ignore traditional outlets:

- Local newspapers and TV: Pitch your book as a local success story. Or better yet, tie your book to a current headline or cultural topic, if you can. In the media industry, this is called tying it to a news peg.
- Radio interviews: Many stations are eager to feature local authors. (And in the proliferation of podcasts and online shows, radio sometimes gets overlooked. Radio programming is always looking for relevant content.)
- Libraries and bookstores: Arrange signings or launch parties.

A hybrid strategy—digital and physical—often brings the best results.

Launch Events

Events give your book launch a face-to-face dimension. They can be in-person or virtual.

In-Person Ideas:

- Bookstore signing.
- Library talk.
- Book-themed party at a café or community center. When my first book *Sometimes Art Can't Save You,* published in 2005, we held a release party at a local Mexican restaurant by renting it out on the one night they closed each week and where the owners had become our friends. They were thrilled to host it and to make money on their night off. My husband and I invited all of our colleagues and friends, and dozens of people came—including some from out of state— to enjoy margaritas, nachos, and mini-enchiladas; to have me sign copies of their books; and to celebrate the

book's release and my success. I painted a replica of the book's front cover on canvas and placed it on an easel at the entrance of the restaurant to add to the decor. When you host events away from the usual venues of bookstores, the atmosphere can be more fun and lively, which makes people want to join in the festivities.

Virtual Ideas:

- Online launch party with giveaways.
- Author Q&A via Zoom or Facebook Live or on reddit.
- Collaborative event with other authors.

Make your event interactive: trivia, games, or live readings can keep audiences engaged.

Post-Launch Momentum

Launch week isn't the end—it's the beginning of your book's life. After the initial flurry:

1. Track results: Which posts, emails, or events worked best?
2. Keep promoting: Share reviews, new content, or bonus material weekly.
3. Thank supporters: Personalized notes to reviewers and street team members go a long way.
4. Plan a second wave: Around 3–4 weeks post-launch, plan a fresh campaign to keep sales going.

Post-launch is also the time you will continue to do guest blogging and radio, tv, print media, and podcast interviews, as well as bookstore events. These, plus speaking engagements, may go on for months. When two of my books, *Sometimes*

Art Can't Save You (2005) and *Creating the Freelance Career* (2018) released, I did interviews and I wrote guest blogs for almost a year after in each case, as well as university and store readings and speaking engagements and signings. Being able to create this kind of longer momentum increases book sales and helps promote you as a brand.

Let's look at three short case studies to see how Colleen Hoover, Sarah J. Maas, and Chris Fox handled their book launches.

 CASE STUDY:
The Power of a Coordinated Launch

Indie romance author Colleen Hoover provides one of the clearest examples of how a well-planned launch strategy can propel an author from obscurity to global success. Hoover self-published her debut novel *Slammed* in January 2012, originally intending it only for friends and family. But within six months, it had become a bestseller—largely because of how she leveraged early readers, online communities, and carefully timed promotion.

What She Did Right

1. Built a Community Before Fame
Hoover joined Goodreads groups, indie author forums, and book blogging communities where readers were eager to discover fresh voices. Instead of spamming "buy my book" messages, she shared genuine stories, engaged in conversations, and built relationships. This laid the groundwork for a supportive community that was ready to share her work when it launched.

2. Early Reviews as Social Proof

By providing advance copies to influential book bloggers, Hoover created early buzz. Those reviews gave her debut credibility and encouraged hesitant readers to give it a chance. Many cited this social proof as a key reason for trying a new author.

3. Strategic Use of E-Book Pricing

Hoover priced her ebook at $2.99—an accessible price point that reduced risk for new readers. Combined with her positive reviews, this led to a surge in downloads, which in turn boosted her book into Amazon's recommendation algorithms.

4. Engaging Directly With Readers

She didn't wait for readers to find her—she actively engaged them. Hoover responded to Goodreads reviews, interacted with fans on Facebook, and made readers feel like insiders on her journey. Readers who felt personally connected became her strongest advocates, often posting word-of-mouth recommendations that reached thousands more.

5. Layered Promotions

Hoover didn't rely on a single tactic. She ran giveaways, posted teasers, hosted Q&As, and asked readers to share their favorite quotes. This multi-pronged approach kept momentum going throughout launch week and beyond.

Long-Term Impact

The success of *Slammed* and its sequel led to a publishing deal with Atria Books (a Simon & Schuster imprint), catapulting Hoover into the mainstream. Even after signing with a traditional publisher, she has continued to use grassroots strategies—exclusive reader groups, CoHorts street teams, and social media challenges—to create excitement before every launch.

By 2022, Hoover had become the best-selling novelist in the United States, outselling even major household names. Her career trajectory shows that launch strategy isn't just about one book—it's about cultivating readers who will eagerly return for the next release.

 **Key Takeaways for Authors**

- Don't wait until launch week to connect with readers— start months (or years) earlier.
- Use advance reviews and endorsements to build credibility before launch.
- Price strategically to remove barriers for new readers.
- Engage authentically; personal interaction can turn casual readers into lifelong fans.
- Plan for layered, ongoing promotion—launch week is only the spark.

Hoover's story illustrates how a coordinated, reader-centered launch can make all the difference. She didn't have a huge budget, a famous name, or a big publishing house behind her in the beginning. What she did have was strategy, authenticity, and the willingness to put readers first.

 CASE STUDY:
Sarah J. Maas – Leveraging Social Media & Global Fandom

Fantasy author Sarah J. Maas shows how social media can amplify launch week on a global scale. By the time her first book in the *Throne of Glass* series launched, Maas had begun interacting with fans via Tumblr, early Twitter communities, and fan blogs.

For her later launches, she utilized Instagram, TikTok, and Goodreads to create buzz with cover reveals, countdowns, and sneak-peek chapters. Maas also ran hashtag campaigns, encouraging fans to post fan art, quotes, and reactions. This strategy tapped into the enthusiasm of an already passionate audience and generated massive visibility, particularly among younger fantasy readers who rely heavily on social platforms for book discovery.

Her launch weeks often include interactive events, such as Q&As, live readings, and exclusive giveaways. Fans worldwide synchronize their online activity, posting reviews, unboxing videos, and fan content simultaneously, creating a viral effect.

 ## Key Takeaways for Authors

* Harness social media to connect with global audiences.
* Use fan participation to amplify visibility.
* Interactive campaigns and content sharing can create a viral launch effect.

 ## CASE STUDY:
Chris Fox – Local and Indie-Focused Strategy

Author Chris Fox, known for his self-published science fiction and writing guides, demonstrates the power of a more traditional, location-based launch strategy. Fox emphasizes building relationships with independent bookstores, libraries, and writing groups. His launch weeks include:

- In-person book signings and readings at local bookstores.
- Partnerships with library reading clubs and local events.
- Email campaigns targeted at readers who purchased his previous books.

Fox's strategy shows that a strong launch doesn't require going viral online. By cultivating local support and leveraging direct communication with a loyal audience, he creates concentrated sales bursts that boost visibility on online platforms, while also building lasting personal connections with readers.

 ## Key Takeaways for Authors

- Local networks can drive meaningful book sales.
- Direct, personal engagement builds loyalty.
- Not every author needs to focus on social media virality; in-person strategy can be highly effective.

Summary of Case Study Lessons

- Colleen Hoover: Community-building and grassroots engagement can make a small self-published book explode onto the bestseller lists.
- Sarah J. Maas: Social media and global fandom engagement can create viral momentum, especially for genres with young, enthusiastic audiences.
- Chris Fox: Local events and direct relationships can generate strong sales without relying on online virality.

These three examples highlight that there isn't a single formula for launch week success. The right strategy depends on your genre, audience, resources, and personality. What matters most is planning ahead, engaging readers, and creating momentum that lasts beyond the first week.

 ## QUICK CHECKLIST:
Launch Week

- Have I created a launch schedule with daily focus points?
- Is my street team ready with materials and instructions?
- Do I have graphics, teasers, and giveaways prepared in advance?
- Have I reached out to the media and bloggers? (Or hired a publicist to handle this for me?)
- Do I have a plan to sustain momentum after week one?

 ## Summary

- Launch week is critical for visibility, algorithms, and momentum.
- Preparation is key: reviewers, street teams, and assets must be ready.
- Use a day-by-day plan to keep engagement high.
- Mix digital strategies with local and traditional media.
- Treat launch week as a celebration—your enthusiasm is contagious.

References:

- Bowker. (2020). "Self-Publishing in the United States, 2014–2019."
- Nielsen Book Research. (2019). "Understanding the Book Buyer."

CHAPTER 8
MARKETING BEYOND LAUNCH WEEK: THE LONG GAME

Congratulations! Your launch week is over, your book is out in the world, and your street team has done its job. You might be tempted to sit back and relax—and take a nap that lasts a week. But here's the truth: the work of marketing a book doesn't end when launch week does. Launch week and the weeks or months leading up to it are just the beginning.

Sustained marketing is what keeps your book visible, attracts new readers, and builds a long-term career as an author. This chapter is about the long game: strategies that ensure your book keeps selling months and years after publication.

Why the Long Game Matters

A strong launch can give your book a big spike in sales, but without ongoing marketing, it can quickly fade from view. According to Nielsen Book Research (2019), books with consistent post-launch promotion sell "30–50% more copies over the first year" than those left to rely solely on the launch buzz.

Think of your marketing as a garden: launch week is planting, but post-launch marketing is watering, weeding, and nurturing growth so the book flourishes over time.

Build an Email Marketing System

If you haven't already, now is the time to invest in your mailing list. Your email list is your most direct line to readers. Unlike social media, which is subject to algorithms, email goes straight to the inbox.

Best Practices for email marketing includes:

1. **Regular Updates:** Send a monthly or biweekly newsletter with book updates, exclusive content, or personal insights.
2. **Segment Your Audience:** Separate subscribers by genre interest, previous purchases, or engagement level for tailored messaging.
3. **Provide Value:** Offer free chapters, behind-the-scenes content, or writing tips in addition to book announcements.
4. **Call-to-Action:** Encourage subscribers to share your book, leave reviews, or participate in events.

Even after launch, nurturing your email list keeps readers engaged for your next release.

Consistent Social Media Engagement

You don't need to post every day, but consistency matters. Ongoing social media activity keeps your book discoverable.

Content Ideas Beyond Launch:

- Weekly or Monthly Highlights: Quotes, excerpts, or favorite scenes.
- Reader Spotlights: Share photos of readers enjoying your book.
- Writing Process Updates: Give fans insight into your next project.
- Collaborations: Cross-promote with other authors in your genre.

Remember the 80/20 rule from Chapter 5: 80% engagement, 20% promotion. Authentic interaction matters more than sheer volume.

Seasonal & Themed Promotions

Books often benefit from tie-ins to events, holidays, or cultural moments.

- Holiday Sales: Christmas, Valentine's Day, or back-to-school promotions.
- Awareness Days: Tie your book to relevant themes— National Poetry Month, Women's History Month, etc.
- Genre Celebrations: Fantasy, sci-fi, or romance events online.

Planning a few mini-campaigns throughout the year keeps your book visible without exhausting your energy.

Leverage Reviews Continuously

Reviews aren't just for launch week. New reviews posted months after release help keep your book credible and discoverable.

- Encourage readers to leave honest reviews when they finish the book.
- Feature fresh reviews on your website or social media.
- Reach out to bloggers and influencers for seasonal review opportunities.

A steady stream of reviews signals to both readers and algorithms that your book is active.

Events and Book Clubs

Maintaining a presence in the real world keeps your book alive:

- Book Clubs: Offer discussion guides, Q&A sessions, or virtual appearances.
- Library Talks & Author Events: Schedule appearances at local libraries or community centers.
- Workshops: If your book has a nonfiction element, teach mini-classes or webinars related to your topic.

Even small, recurring events strengthen your long-term sales and deepen reader relationships.

Collaborations & Partnerships

Partnering with other authors or creators can extend your reach:

- **Joint Giveaways:** Combine audiences for mutual benefit.
- **Guest Blog Posts / Podcasts:** Introduce your book to a wider audience.
- **Anthologies or Box Sets:** Work with authors in your genre to reach new readers.

Collaboration keeps your marketing fresh and opens doors that single-author campaigns may miss.

Marketing Your Book to Book Clubs

Book clubs are more than just a gathering of readers—they're micro-communities where stories are discussed, shared, and recommended. A single club can influence dozens of readers (and their networks) because members often go on to recommend books to friends, family, and co-workers. Word-of-mouth from a passionate reader carries enormous weight, and authors who learn how to connect with these groups can see a ripple effect that grows far beyond one meeting.

Why Book Clubs Matter

- **Built-in audience:** Book clubs buy multiple copies of books at once.
- **Deeper engagement:** Club members don't just read—they dissect themes, characters, and writing. This builds loyalty to the author.
- **Amplification potential:** If a book resonates, members often spread the word outside the group.

- **Celebrity club endorsements:** Oprah's Book Club and Reese's Book Club have turned several titles into megahits (Delia Owens, Celeste Ng, Tayari Jones).

How to Market Your Book to Book Clubs

1. Create a Book Club Kit

- Provide discussion questions, author insights, and even playlists or recipes tied to your book.
- Make it downloadable from your website. This extra resource makes it easier for club leaders to select your book.

2. Offer Virtual or In-Person Author Visits

- Many clubs love the opportunity to chat with an author. Offering free 15–30 minute Q&A sessions via Zoom can help you build lifelong fans. I've done a number of these and they are a lot of fun as many people have never had the chance to talk personally to the author of a book they have read.

3. Target Local Clubs First

- Libraries, bookstores, and community centers often have lists of active book clubs. Reach out and introduce your book, offering copies at a discount or donating a set to get conversations started.

4. Leverage Social Media for Clubs

- Goodreads, Facebook Groups, and sites like BookClubz.com allow you to connect directly with organizers who are always on the hunt for engaging reads.
- Be authentic—pitch your book in a way that emphasizes why it makes a good discussion piece.

5. Encourage Word-of-Mouth Marketing

- Incentivize readers with shareable graphics or even small giveaways for those who recommend your book to another club.
- Some authors mail signed bookplates to members, creating a personal connection without the expense of shipping full books.

6. Partner with Bookstores and Libraries

- Many host regular book club events and are eager for author collaborations. You could pitch your book as a featured title, offer to attend a session, or suggest a co-hosted event.

 ## CASE STUDY:
Andy Weir – From Self-Published Novelist to Global Bestseller

Andy Weir, the author of *The Martian*, provides an excellent example of how sustained, strategic post-launch marketing can transform a self-published book into a mainstream phenomenon. His approach demonstrates the power of continuous audience engagement, leveraging communities, and using free or low-cost promotional tactics to build momentum over time.

1. Starting with a Niche Audience

Weir initially wrote *The Martian* chapter by chapter and posted it for free on his personal website in 2009. This early approach allowed him to:

- Connect with science and engineering enthusiasts, who

were his target readers.
- Receive direct feedback on scientific accuracy, which he incorporated into revisions.
- Build a small but highly engaged fanbase before any formal book launch.

By offering content for free initially, Weir created trust and goodwill, making readers invested in his story long before it became a commercial product.

Lesson: Early engagement with a niche audience establishes credibility and builds word-of-mouth before formal publication.

2. Leveraging Online Communities

Weir actively engaged with forums such as Reddit's /r/space and /r/science, as well as fan blogs dedicated to space exploration and science fiction. Key aspects of his strategy included:

- Responding to reader comments directly to create a sense of community.
- Sharing drafts, clarifying scientific concepts, and fostering discussion around the story.
- Encouraging readers to share chapters with friends, effectively creating organic promotion channels.

These communities acted as early advocates, spreading the book to like-minded readers and creating momentum that extended beyond Weir's personal reach.

Lesson: Targeted online communities can amplify your book's reach and serve as early promoters if you engage authentically.

3. Transitioning to Self-Publishing

After receiving encouragement from his online readers, Weir self-published *The Martian* as an e-book on Amazon in 2011 for 99 cents. This low price removed barriers to purchase and allowed word-of-mouth to flourish.

- Early reviews on Amazon highlighted the book's unique blend of hard science and humor, attracting more readers.
- Social sharing and email recommendations from his existing fanbase created an initial surge in downloads.
- Amazon's algorithm picked up on consistent sales, further increasing visibility in search results and recommendation lists.

Lesson: Affordable pricing and strong early reviews can significantly boost algorithmic visibility, particularly on e-book platforms.

4. Maintaining Post-Launch Engagement

Unlike many authors who rely solely on launch week, Weir continued to engage his readers months and years after publication. He updated the book based on reader feedback to correct minor errors, signaling responsiveness (rewrites and changes of more than 25 percent require new ISBN. He shared insights about the writing process, Mars science, and other related topics on his website and social media. And he participated in interviews, podcasts, and live Q&A sessions, keeping the book visible in the media.

Lesson: Continuous engagement keeps a book alive and discoverable long after its initial release.

5. Expansion and Traditional Publishing

The sustained attention from his fanbase attracted traditional publishers. Weir signed with Crown Publishing, who released a print edition in 2014. By this point, *The Martian* had already built:

- A dedicated fan community.
- Positive reviews and word-of-mouth momentum.
- Media interest from science and tech outlets due to the book's realistic portrayal of Mars colonization.

This pre-existing traction made the book an easier sell for publishers and set the stage for mainstream success.

6. Film Adaptation and Global Reach

Ridley Scott's 2015 film adaptation of *The Martian* skyrocketed Weir's book sales globally. However, the groundwork for this success was laid by years of strategic engagement and sustained visibility, not a single viral moment. Fans who had read the book early became advocates for the film, sharing it online and generating buzz. Weir's engagement with both science communities and general audiences bridged the niche-to-mainstream gap.

Lesson: Long-term marketing and audience-building efforts can create opportunities for adaptation, translation, and cross-media success.

 **Key Takeaways from Andy Weir's Strategy**

1. Build an early, invested audience by offering free or low-cost content.

2. Engage directly with niche communities to amplify word-of-mouth.
3. Use early reviews and feedback to improve visibility and credibility.
4. Maintain ongoing engagement post-launch to sustain momentum.
5. Leverage community-driven success to attract publishers and media opportunities.
6. Plan for long-term growth, not just initial sales.

Andy Weir's approach demonstrates that even a self-published author with no initial platform can achieve global recognition with a consistent, strategic long-term marketing mindset. His success reinforces the idea that launch week is only the beginning—sustained engagement and community cultivation are what turn a single book into a career-defining success.

Detailed Steps of What Andy Weir Did:

2009 – Website Posting
- Weir posts The Martian chapter by chapter on his personal website.
- Engages directly with early readers.
- Receives feedback on scientific accuracy.
- Builds a small, dedicated fanbase.

2011 – Self-Publishing on Amazon
- Publishes the full e-book for $0.99.
- Leverages early fanbase to generate initial downloads.
- Encourages reviews and sharing to expand reach.
- Book gains traction through Amazon's recommendation algorithms.

2011–2013 – Post-Launch Engagement

- Responds to reader comments and questions online.
- Shares updates, insights, and corrections on the book.
- Participates in forums and online communities (Reddit, science blogs).
- Sustains visibility and builds loyalty over time.

2014 – Traditional Publishing Deal
- Signs with Crown Publishing for print and expanded distribution.
- Pre-existing fanbase makes the book attractive to publishers.
- Reviews, media attention, and audience engagement help boost print sales.

2015 – Film Adaptation & Global Success
- Ridley Scott directs *The Martian* film adaptation, starring Matt Damon.
- Book gains mainstream attention and international readership.
- Sustained marketing, community engagement, and credibility lead to cross-media success.

 **Key Takeaways from Timeline:**

1. Early engagement can create a fanbase before formal publication.
2. Low-cost or free content is an investment in reader loyalty.
3. Sustained post-launch engagement prolongs momentum.
4. Strategic growth attracts traditional publishers and media opportunities.
5. Long-term planning can result in mainstream recognition and adaptations.

Avoiding the "One-Hit Wonder" Trap

Many authors experience a spike in launch week excitement but fail to maintain visibility. Common pitfalls:

- **Neglecting readers after launch:** Without ongoing communication, your audience forgets.
- **Ignoring social media completely:** Even occasional posts keep your book discoverable.
- **Failing to plan ahead:** Post-launch promotions are easier when you schedule them in advance.

The antidote: consistent, manageable marketing that fits your schedule and personality.

 QUICK CHECKLIST: Long-Term Marketing

1. Do I have an active email list with regular updates?
2. Am I posting on social media consistently and authentically?
3. Do I plan seasonal promotions or themed campaigns?
4. Am I actively encouraging reviews beyond launch week?
5. 5. Do I participate in book clubs, events, or collaborations to maintain visibility?

 **Summary**

- Marketing beyond launch week ensures lasting visibility and sales.
- Email newsletters, social media, seasonal campaigns, and events sustain engagement.
- Collaborations, guest appearances, and continuous

review collection reinforce credibility.
- Consistency, authenticity, and planning are key to building a long-term author career.

Marketing isn't a sprint—it's a marathon. By nurturing readers, keeping your book in front of new audiences, and celebrating milestones along the way, your book can continue to thrive long after launch week.

References:

- Nielsen Book Research. (2019). "Understanding the Book Buyer."
- Bowker. (2020). "Self-Publishing in the United States, 2014–2019."

CHAPTER 9
PAID MARKETING AND ADS: WHEN AND HOW TO INVEST

U p to now, we've focused on organic marketing strategies: building an audience, leveraging reviews, engaging with fans, and maximizing launch week. But sometimes, the fastest way to reach new readers is through paid marketing. Ads, when done strategically, can give your book visibility you can't achieve organically—without breaking the bank.

This chapter covers the basics of paid marketing, how to choose the right platforms, and how to maximize return on investment.

Why Paid Marketing Can Work

Organic marketing—social media posts, newsletters, word-of-mouth—works well for loyal readers, but it has limits. Paid marketing allows you to:

1. Reach new readers quickly: Ads target people who may not know you exist.
2. Target specific audiences: Platforms let you define demographics, interests, or behaviors.
3. Scale effectively: Ads can be adjusted to fit almost any budget.

According to a 2021 Author Earnings report, indie authors who combined organic marketing with even modest ad spend often saw a 25–40% increase in sales within the first month of a campaign. Ads can be bought directly on platforms or if you have published your book through printer and distributor IngramSparks, you can buy social media ads directly on their platform.

Choosing the Right Platform

Not all ad platforms work equally well for every book or audience. Here's a breakdown:

1. Amazon Ads
- Best for: Direct book sales on Amazon.
- How it works: You can run Sponsored Product, Sponsored Brand, or Lockscreen ads targeting keywords or competitor books.

Tips:
- Start small ($5–$10/day) to test keywords.
- Monitor click-through rates (CTR) and conversion rates.
- Adjust keywords based on performance; eliminate underperforming ones.

2. Facebook & Instagram Ads

- Best for: Building awareness and driving traffic to your book or newsletter.
- How it works: Ads can be highly targeted by demographics, interests, and behaviors.

Tips:

- Use eye-catching images or video snippets.
- Test multiple versions ("A/B testing") to see which creatives perform best.
- Focus on building your email list as well as selling books.

[If you are unfamiliar with A/B testing, this is what it is: A/B testing for ads is like running a little experiment to see what people like better. You make two versions of the same ad—say, one shows your book cover on a cozy reading chair, and the other shows it on a coffee shop table. Everything else about the ads stays the same. You run both at the same time, and the platform (like Facebook or Instagram) shows each version to different groups of people. Then you compare the results: Did more people click on the ad with the reading chair, or the coffee shop? By testing one change at a time, you learn what grabs attention and helps sell your book without wasting money on guesses.]

3. BookBub Ads

(If you don't know BookBub, it is a platform where readers can choose discounted price e-books in genres of their choosing. BookBub sends readers a daily email listing free and discounted books in whatever genres they said in their registration that they read and then when the reader clicks the link, it takes them to that book on Amazon.)

- Best for: Genre fiction, especially romance, thriller, fantasy, and sci-fi.
- How it works: Promotes your book to readers who have expressed interest in similar titles.

Tips:
- Strong covers and blurbs are essential—BookBub readers scroll fast.
- Start with short campaigns to test results before scaling.

4. TikTok Ads
- Best for: YA, fantasy, romance, and books appealing to younger (often under ages 35- 40) audiences.
- How it works: Short video ads appear in users' feeds.

Tips:
- Keep videos 10–30 seconds with clear messaging.
- Engage with trends and hashtags to increase organic amplification.

Setting Your Budget

Paid marketing doesn't have to be expensive. Even $50–$100 per month can yield measurable results if campaigns are carefully targeted. Some of the platforms, like Facebook and Amazon, allow you to set daily spend limits. Others, like BookBub, are one-time spends, such as $800 to run a special on your book to their thousands of daily newsletter recipients.

Budgeting tips:

- Start small, monitor results, and scale gradually.
- Allocate more to campaigns that show positive ROI.

- Track metrics like Click-Thru Rates (CTR), conversion rates, and cost per sale.

Think of your ad spend like an experiment: small, data-driven steps prevent wasted money.

Crafting Effective Ads

A great ad has three elements:

1. **Attention**-grabbing visual or headline – Your cover, a quote, or a short video snippet.
2. **Compelling copy** – Explain why someone should read your book in 1–2 sentences. Highlight a hook, genre, or benefit.
3. **Clear call-to-action (CTA)** – "Buy now," "Read a free sample," or "Sign up for my newsletter."

Example:

Headline: "A Gripping Thriller You Can't Put Down"
Image: Book cover with a suspenseful visual.
CTA: "Start reading today on Kindle!"

Testing and Optimizing

Ads are rarely perfect the first time. Track performance metrics, then adjust:

- CTR (Click-Through Rate): Are people clicking your ad? If low, tweak the visual or headline.
- Conversion Rate: Are clicks turning into purchases? If low, revise your landing page or Amazon or Ingram description.

- Cost Per Acquisition: How much are you spending per sale? Aim to stay profitable.

Run multiple small campaigns rather than a single large one. Testing allows you to find what resonates with your audience without overspending.

When Paid Marketing Makes Sense

Paid marketing works best when:

- You have a ready product with a polished cover, blurb, and professional formatting.
- Your organic marketing is established, so ads amplify rather than compensate for zero visibility.
- You have a defined target audience—you know who your readers are and where they spend time online.

Avoid spending money on ads if your book isn't fully ready, your website or purchase links aren't functional, or your target audience isn't clearly defined.

 ## CASE STUDY:
Hanna James & Facebook Ads

Indie romance author Hanna James demonstrates how a small, well-targeted ad budget can yield significant results when executed strategically.

Background

Hannah James self-publishes contemporary romance novels. Before exploring paid advertising, she relied primarily on social media engagement, email newsletters, and organic word-of-mouth. While her existing readers were loyal, she wanted to reach new audiences without relying solely on viral moments or costly PR campaigns.

Her Strategy:

1. Defined Target Audience:
James identified her ideal readers by analyzing who purchased similar books on Amazon and which social media groups her current fans frequented. She focused on women ages 18–45 with interests in romance fiction, specific subgenres (e.g., small-town romance), and followings of similar authors.

2. Crafted Compelling Ads:
She tested multiple ad creatives:

Image-based ads: Showcasing her book cover with a romantic, visually striking backdrop.
Text-based ads: Short emotional hooks like, "Fall in love with a story that will make your heart race and your cheeks blush."
Video snippets: 15–20 second teasers with narrated excerpts and soft music, giving a sense of the book's tone.

3. Audience Segmentation and Testing:
She ran three small campaigns simultaneously, each targeting a slightly different audience segment:

- Fans of competitor authors.
- Followers of romance-related social media groups.
- General readers who had shown interest in book giveaways or e-book promotions.

4. Budget Management:
James started with a modest budget of $50/day per campaign.

She tracked metrics closely: click-through rates, conversions (actual book purchases), and cost per acquisition. After a week, she cut the lowest-performing segment and doubled the budget for the best-performing one.

5. Optimizing Landing Pages:
She made sure her Amazon book pages, newsletter sign-ups, and website landing pages were optimized. Compelling blurbs, clear calls-to-action, and a strong cover image ensured that the traffic driven by ads converted effectively into sales.

The Results

- Hanna James saw a 300% return on ad spend (ROAS) within two weeks.
- Her best-performing ad—targeting fans of a similar romance author—converted clicks into sales at $0.80 per acquisition, which is exceptionally cost-effective in indie publishing.
- Beyond immediate sales, the campaigns increased newsletter sign-ups, giving James a growing list of engaged readers for future releases.

 **Key Takeaways for Authors**

1. Ad copy matters as much as targeting. A short, emotionally engaging hook outperformed flashy visuals alone.
2. Audience segmentation pays off. Testing small campaigns with different segments allowed Hanna to optimize her spend and maximize conversions.
3. Optimize the "post-click" experience. Even the best ads fail if the book page isn't compelling, so Hanna ensured covers, blurbs, and reviews were strong.

4. Budget small, scale smart. Starting modestly minimizes risk, while monitoring metrics ensures money is only spent on high-performing campaigns.

Hanna James' success shows that paid marketing doesn't require huge budgets or a viral TikTok moment. Careful targeting, testing, and optimization—even with modest funds—can dramatically expand your reach, boost sales, and build a longer-term reader base. Paid campaigns work best as a complement to your organic marketing efforts, reinforcing visibility and credibility in a competitive marketplace.

Pitfalls to Avoid

- Skipping the testing phase: Don't throw money at ads without monitoring results.
- Targeting too broadly: Wasting impressions on uninterested users drains your budget.
- Ignoring your ROI: Always calculate cost per sale to ensure your campaigns are profitable.
- Neglecting your landing page or book description: If the ad gets clicks but your Amazon page isn't compelling, sales will stall.

 QUICK CHECKLIST: Paid Marketing

1. Have I polished my book cover, blurb, and product page?
2. Do I have a defined target audience for my ads?
3. Have I started with small campaigns to test visuals, copy, and platforms?
4. Am I tracking CTR, conversion, and cost per sale?
5. Do I have a plan to scale campaigns that are profitable?

 **Summary**

- Paid marketing accelerates visibility and sales when done strategically.
- Choose the platform that aligns with your book and audience.
- Start small, test, and optimize campaigns for best results.
- Track ROI and avoid overspending on untested ads.
- Paid marketing works best as a complement to strong organic marketing.

Paid advertising is not a magic bullet—but when used wisely, it can help your book reach readers who would otherwise never know it exists. With careful targeting, testing, and consistent monitoring, paid campaigns can become a powerful tool in your marketing toolkit.

References:

- Author Earnings. (2021). "Indie Authors and Digital Marketing Report."
- Nielsen Book Research. (2019). "Understanding the Book Buyer."

CHAPTER 10
AUTHOR BRANDING AND LONG-TERM CAREER STRATEGY

I f paid marketing, launch week, and social media engagement are the tools of book marketing, author branding is the foundation. Your brand is how readers perceive you, how they remember your books, and how they choose to follow your career. A strong brand creates trust, builds loyalty, and makes every marketing effort more effective.

This chapter explores what author branding is, how to cultivate it, and how to turn each book release into a stepping stone for a long-term career.

What is Author Branding?

Your author brand is the sum of:

- **Your voice and style:** How you write, the tone you use, and the themes you explore.
- **Your online presence:** Website, social media, newsletters, and public persona.
- **Your reputation:** How readers perceive your professionalism, engagement, and authenticity.
- **Consistency across works:** Genre, themes, and cover aesthetics that make your books recognizable.

Think of your brand as the "person behind the books" that readers get to know, trust, and recommend. It's not about being famous—it's about being memorable, approachable, and consistent. Let's explore how to build your author brand. I believe every author should have one and should be intentional about telling the world who they are.

Building Your Author Brand

1. Define Your Niche
- Identify your genre, themes, or writing style.
- Consider what makes your stories unique.
- Think about the type of readers you want to attract.
-

Example: If you write cozy mysteries with strong female protagonists, your brand might emphasize humor, small-town charm, and clever sleuthing. Readers should recognize your books and marketing materials as part of a cohesive identity.

2. Create a Consistent Visual Identity
Logo, font choices, and color schemes for your website and

social media.

- Cover design consistency across a series or multiple books in the same genre.
- Consistent photo style if using author portraits.

Consistency builds recognition—if a reader sees your book or post, they should immediately think, That's a [Your Name] book!

3. Develop Your Online Presence

- **Website:** Central hub for your books, newsletter sign-ups, and blog posts.The URL can be your name, or if you are writing a book series, the name of the series—or in many cases, it is smart to buy both your name and your book series name URL as that gives you complete legal and creative control over your brand and your books. Even when I've published with traditional publishers, I've always bought a URL attached to my book and built out its website. And don't forget to add a blog or other parts of your website that get regularly updated. This is one way your site arrives at and stays on page one of search engines.
- **Social Media:** Choose platforms where your readers hang out. Maintain consistent posting and tone.
- **Newsletter:** Regular updates keep readers engaged between releases.

Tip: Authenticity matters more than perfection. Readers respond to authors who are approachable and relatable.

To help you zero in on your personal brand, here's a guided exercise I've used with authors that helps clarify their brand. It's practical, reflective, and gets them thinking about how they show up to readers:

Author Branding Exercise: "The Three Circles of You"

Step 1: Your Core (Circle One: Who You Are)
Write down 5–7 words that describe you as a person beyond writing.

- What values matter most to you? (e.g., curiosity, kindness, resilience, humor)
- What parts of your personality do people notice right away?
- If readers met you in person, what impression would you want them to leave with?

Example: adventurous, empathetic, coffee-obsessed, playful, disciplined, optimistic.

Step 2: Your Work (Circle Two: What You Write)
Write down 5–7 words or phrases that describe your writing itself.

- What themes show up often in your work? (e.g., redemption, love, justice, community)
- How would readers describe the experience of reading your books? (e.g., cozy, fast-paced, lyrical, funny, suspenseful)
- What genres do you write in, and what sets your work apart?

Example: heartfelt, character-driven, humorous, small-town, hopeful, mystery with a dash of danger.

Step 3: Your Readers (Circle Three: Who You Serve)
Now think about your audience.

- Who do you imagine when you picture your "ideal reader"?

- What do they love about your books—or about books in general?
- What kind of community or feeling do you want them to have around your author brand?

Example: middle-aged women who love dogs, book clubs who enjoy cozy mysteries, readers who want a comforting escape after a long day.

Step 4: Find the Overlap
Look at all three circles. Where do they overlap? That's the sweet spot of your personal brand. This is where your personality, your writing style/themes, and your readers' desires all come together.

Example brand statement: "I'm a cozy mystery author who brings humor, heart, and a love of small-town quirks to readers who want comfort with a twist of intrigue."

Step 5: Put It Into Practice
Answer these quick prompts to turn your brand into action:

1. **Visuals:** What colors, fonts, or images reflect your brand's tone?
2. **Voice:** What words or phrases do you want to consistently use when you talk to readers?
3. **Promises:** What do you want readers to know they'll always get from your books?

Goal: By the end of this exercise, you should have a one-sentence brand statement and a few guidelines that help you show up consistently in your website, social media, and book marketing.

Turning Each Book into a Career Step

Instead of treating each book as an isolated project, think of it as part of a long-term trajectory.

1. Cross-Promotion
- Reference your previous books in your new releases.
- Offer boxed sets or series promotions.
- Use newsletters to announce sequels, prequels, or related works.

2. Audience Retention
- Keep readers engaged between releases with behind-the-scenes content, short stories, or interactive events.
- Engage with your street team and loyal readers regularly.

3. Career Planning
- Map out your book releases strategically—genre consistency helps readers know what to expect.
- Consider multiple revenue streams: print, ebooks, audiobooks, and translations.
- Build a brand that attracts partnerships: guest posts, podcasts, speaking engagements, or collaborations.

Long-Term Marketing Mindset

While launch weeks and ad campaigns are important, the most sustainable marketing strategy is long-term consistency in your brand and your offerings. This means you should maintain regular content on your website, newsletter, and social media. You can plan mini-campaigns around holidays or events each year. And you continually need to collect reviews and engage your audience to keep your books visible.

Authors who succeed over years—not just weeks—treat every marketing effort as cumulative. Your audience grows, your visibility increases, and your brand strengthens with each book.

CASE STUDY: Brandon Sanderson – Building a Career, Not Just Books

Yes, we are going to look at Brandon Sanderson one more time because he is a prime example of an author who approaches writing as a long-term career, rather than focusing solely on individual book sales. His success is rooted in consistent branding, audience engagement, and strategic planning. Let's break down how he does it and what lessons we can draw for authors at any stage.

1. Consistency in Genre and Style

From the beginning of his career, Sanderson has been known for epic fantasy novels with detailed world-building, intricate magic systems, and multi-layered plots. Readers know exactly what to expect when they pick up a Sanderson book. This predictability reinforces trust in his brand.

Lesson for authors: Define your niche and deliver consistently. Your readers should be able to identify your style across multiple books.

2. Strategic Release Planning

Sanderson doesn't release books randomly. He plans series releases and stand-alone novels years in advance, often staggering books in ways that maintain reader engagement without overwhelming them. For example:

- A book in the *Mistborn* series might be released one year.
- The next year sees a different series or a stand-alone novel.
- Special events, like short stories or novellas, fill in gaps and maintain momentum.

This approach keeps fans engaged continuously while building a larger universe around his books.

Lesson for authors: Map out releases to maintain visibility and keep your readers anticipating the next title.

3. Community Engagement and Accessibility
Sanderson is exceptionally active in engaging with his fans:

- Maintains an active newsletter, sharing writing insights, sneak peeks, and updates.
- Participates in podcasts, interviews, and online forums.
- Hosts events such as live Q&As and fan conventions.

By connecting directly with readers, he builds loyalty and trust—fans feel personally invested in his career.

Lesson for authors: Regular, authentic interaction with your audience strengthens your brand and encourages word-of-mouth marketing.

4. Multi-Platform Presence
Sanderson ensures that his books are available in multiple formats—print, ebook, audiobook, and international editions. (If you are a self-published author, you can find excellent book translators on platforms such as Upwork. I've had my own self-published books translated into Spanish and I've

overseen the translations of my clients' books into very specific languages such as Brazilian Portuguese, Argentinian Spanish, and Hungarian, among others.)

Sanderson also leverages different platforms for visibility:

- Goodreads author page for reviews and reader engagement.
- Social media (Twitter, Instagram, YouTube) to share updates and teasers.
- Online courses and writing advice on his website.

This multi-platform approach maximizes exposure while diversifying revenue streams.

Lesson for authors: Make your work accessible across formats and platforms to reach the widest possible audience.

5. Building a Connected Universe

Sanderson is known for the "Cosmere universe", linking multiple series through shared lore and characters. Even stand-alone books contribute to the larger narrative. This encourages readers to explore more of his work, enhancing lifetime reader value.

Lesson for authors: Consider creating thematic or narrative connections between books to build deeper engagement and repeat readership.

6. Marketing and Branding Integration

Everything Sanderson does—from book covers to website design, event appearances, and newsletter tone—reinforces his brand identity. Fans recognize the style, tone, and quality, which makes promotion more efficient. He rarely has to "sell" each book from scratch; the established brand does much of the work.

7. Results of Long-Term Strategy

- Sanderson has become one of the top-selling fantasy authors worldwide, with millions of books sold.
- Each release benefits from cumulative brand recognition, reducing the effort needed to market individual titles.
- His approach demonstrates that consistent branding, strategic planning, and audience engagement are more valuable than one-off viral success.

 ## Key Takeaways for Authors

1. Consistency in genre, style, and quality builds reader trust.
2. Strategic release schedules maintain momentum and visibility.
3. Direct community engagement fosters loyalty and long-term advocacy.
4. Multi-platform accessibility maximizes reach and revenue.
5. Creating connections between books enhances reader retention and lifetime value.
6. Integrated branding reduces marketing effort per release over time.

Brandon Sanderson's approach shows that a career-focused author strategy—rather than focusing solely on one book's launch—creates exponential growth over time. Even if you're an indie author without a massive audience, applying these principles can gradually build a strong, recognizable brand that sustains your career.

But what if you are an author or want-to-be author who wants to write many different kinds of things? Maybe you are similar to me, and you write nonfiction and fiction, or you want to be like Judy Blume and write books for all age groups. How then do you create your branding so that it seems integrated but also represents the multi-faceted creative that you are?

Let's explore a case study about Mark David Gerson who has written for children and adults, nonfiction and fiction to see how has made him and his branding successful.

Here's a detailed case study of a nonfiction and fiction author who has successfully built a strong personal author brand while writing across multiple genres—embracing versatility rather than shying away from it:

 ## CASE STUDY:
Mark David Gerson – The Storyteller Who Defied Genre

Background

Mark David Gerson is a vibrant example of an author whose brand transcends genre boundaries. He's published more than twenty books, ranging from memoirs and spiritual nonfiction, to fantasy, writing craft guides, and children's parables. Rather than splitting his audience, Gerson unified them under a single compelling identity: he brands himself not by genre, but by his mission—helping people tap into the "transformative power of story".

His Branding Challenges

- **Cross-genre blur:** Fiction readers, self-help readers,

and spiritual seekers don't always overlap.

- **Market expectations:** Retailers and algorithms expect genre consistency.
- **Audience clarity:** Risk of confusing readers or diluting recognition.

Strategic Approach

Gerson navigated these challenges with a cohesive, purpose-driven brand:

1. **Unified Identity**—"I am a storyteller." He doesn't present separate pen names for different genres. Instead, authorship = storytelling. Every book—fiction or nonfiction—fits under that umbrella: whether it's a memoir on healing or a fantasy parable. The mission remains constant.
2. **Audience Expectations Managed Through Messaging**— On his website, social media, and book blurbs, he emphasizes *why* he writes, not just *what* he writes. Readers come for inspiration, creative clarity, and depth—not just genre tropes
3. **Consistent Aesthetic and Voice**—From cover design to newsletter tone, there's a recognizable feel: warm, reflective, visionary. It signals continuity, even when the subject changes
4. **Intentional Platform Use**—Teaching webinars, coaching clients, podcast interviews—all connect back to storytelling. His nonfiction writing reinforces themes from his memoirs; his fiction illustrates them in imaginative ways.

Results & Impact

- **Cross-pollinated readership:** A reader discovering him through a memoir often finds their way into his fantasy or creative writing guides.

- **Platform growth:** His brand identity attracts diverse readers under one umbrella, helping word-of-mouth and retention across genres.
- **Creative freedom:** Gerson is able to follow his curiosity without compromising audience clarity or recognition.

 ## COMPLEMENTARY SHORT CASE STUDY: Mitzi Szereto

Mitzi Szereto is another powerful example of an author who keeps a consistent brand though writing across many genres. She writes across a dizzying range of genres—from cozy mysteries, Gothic horror, true crime anthologies, to parody, sci-fi, erotic fiction, and dark fantasy. A quick look at her Wikipedia page or her website makes this quite clear.

Rather than conceal that breadth, her brand celebrates genre-hopping. Her fans come to expect the eclectic. She's positioned as a genre explorer with a darkly playful sensibility, and each book fits a different corner of that identity.

By branding around voice (edgy, witty, fearless) rather than genre alone, she has built a platform where creativity is part of the draw.

Key Takeaways for Authors
Writing Across Genres

Strategy	Application
Define your thematic mission	Ground your brand in purpose or voice (e.g. storytelling, transformation, wit), not genre.
Be consistent in visuals & tone	Use cohesive cover design elements, fonts, and branding language across projects.
Set clear expectations	Give readers quick context ("This is a creative writing guide," "This is a parable," etc.) so they know what they're getting.
Connect the dots	Use author newsletters, blog posts, or podcasts to talk about the through-line that links your different works.
Own your versatility	If you want to switch genres, do it authentically. Versatility can become a strength if you package it with intention.

Summary

Mark David Gerson illustrates how personal branding—centered on storytelling with heart and integrity—can allow seamless movement across nonfiction, fiction, personal narrative, and craft books. Mitzi Szereto shows that genre-hopping can be an asset when you embrace it with consistency in tone, authorial voice, and fearless creativity.

If you write in multiple genres, you don't need multiple names—you need one clear, authentic brand.

Protecting and Evolving Your Brand

- **Stay authentic:** Don't chase trends that don't align with your writing style or audience.
- **Adapt when necessary:** Platforms, reader interests, and marketing tools change—be ready to evolve.
- **Monitor perception:** Pay attention to feedback from readers and adjust without losing your core identity.

Your brand grows alongside your career. A strong, flexible brand allows you to experiment with new ideas while maintaining reader trust.

 Quick Checklist: Author Branding

1. Have I defined my niche, genre, and writing style?
2. Are my visual and written materials consistent across platforms?
3. Is my website, newsletter, and social media presence maintained regularly?
4. Do I view each book as a step in building a long-term career?

5. Am I engaging with my audience in a consistent, authentic way?

 **Summary**

- Your author brand is your identity, reputation, and consistent presence as a writer.
- Strong branding makes every marketing effort more effective, from launch week to paid ads.
- Plan your book releases as a career strategy, not isolated events.
- Long-term consistency, community engagement, and authenticity create reader loyalty and sustainable success.

Branding is not a one-time effort—it's the lifeblood of your career as an author. By building a strong brand, nurturing your audience, and strategically planning each release, you're not just selling books—you're creating a sustainable, rewarding writing career.

References

- Bowker. (2020). "Self-Publishing in the United States, 2014–2019."
- Author Earnings. (2021). "Indie Authors and Career Development Report."

CHAPTER 11
CREATIVE AND GUERRILLA MARKETING: STANDING OUT IN A CROWDED MARKET

By now, you've learned how to plan your launch, run campaigns, use paid ads, and build a long-term author brand. But sometimes, the best marketing comes from thinking outside the box (or in author-speak, writing beyond the margins). Creative and guerrilla marketing strategies can grab attention, spark word-of-mouth, and make your book memorable—without requiring huge budgets.

This chapter explores innovative ways to promote your book in ways that readers will talk about, share, and remember.

What is Guerrilla Marketing?

Guerrilla marketing is about maximizing impact while minimizing cost. It often relies on creativity, surprise, and audience engagement rather than large advertising budgets.

In the book world, guerrilla marketing can mean:

- Street-level promotions, like posters or flyers in strategic locations.
- Engaging public stunts or pop-up events.
- Highly shareable social media campaigns.

The goal is to create buzz and virality, even with limited resources.

Principles of Creative Marketing

1. **Surprise and Delight** – Give readers something unexpected that captures attention.
2. **Memorability** – Create campaigns that stick in readers' minds.
3. **Shareability** – Design experiences that fans want to share online or in person.
4. **Engagement** – Encourage participation rather than passive observation.

Guerrilla Marketing Tactics for Authors

1. Public Space Engagement
- **Postcards and Flyers:** Place visually appealing postcards in cafes, coffeeshops, libraries, or bookstores. Include QR codes linking to purchase pages or free sample chapters.

- **Book Art Installations:** For fantasy or children's books, create small street installations or book-themed displays that encourage photos. (Make sure you get the necessary permits from the place you live if you need them.)
- **Community Boards:** Leave engaging materials in local businesses or community centers or your local library.

Tip: Make it visually striking and intriguing; don't just leave a plain flyer.

2. Events and Pop-Ups

- **Pop-Up Readings:** Host mini-reading events in unconventional locations—parks, markets, or coffee shops, or even on busy street corners in shopping districts. (Think like a busker for this one. Musicians have employed this tactic for years.)
- **Book Treasure Hunts:** Hide signed copies or swag in your city and post clues online. This encourages reader participation and social sharing.
- **Collaborations with Local Businesses:** Partner with cafés, bookstores, or boutiques to display books or host themed events. When I had an essay published in a dog-theme *Chicken Soup for the Soul* book, I partnered with our local raw food dog manufacturer so that the book would be available in their storefront for purchase, and I left them a few signed copies. They posted about it on their social media channels, which helped drive the sale of the book.

3. Social Media Challenges

- **Hashtag Campaigns:** Create a unique hashtag for your book or series and encourage readers to post pictures, fan art, or reactions.

- Interactive Content: Quizzes, polls, or "choose your adventure" Instagram stories can drive engagement.
- **User-Generated Content:** Offer incentives for readers to create content related to your book. This creates organic promotion.

Example: Romance authors might ask readers to post photos of their most romantic spots around their towns with a hashtag tied to the book.

4. Creative Freebies and Giveaways

- **Branded Merchandise:** Bookmarks, tote bags, or pins featuring quotes or characters.
- **Exclusive Short Stories:** Offer a prequel or side story as a digital download for subscribers.
- **Limited Edition Prints:** Hand-signed pages, sketches, or maps from fantasy novels.

The key is that these items are shareable and collectible, encouraging both engagement and word-of-mouth.

5. Strategic Partnerships

- **Cross-Promotions with Other Authors:** Team up with writers in your genre for joint giveaways or social campaigns.
- **Nonprofit or Community Tie-Ins:** Partner with charities or organizations that align with your book's themes. For example, a historical novel could support a local museum.
- **Local Media Stunts:** Pitch creative stories or events to local newspapers or radio stations to gain free publicity.

CASE STUDY:
Thriller Book in a Box Campaign

The indie thriller author best known for running a successful "book in a box" campaign—and using boxed sets as a launch strategy—is Russell Blake. He collaborated with Melissa Foster and other indie authors to release multi-author thriller bundles, notably the "9 Killer Thrillers" box. This was effectively a "book-in-a-box" campaign—multiple thrillers packaged together at a bargain price to draw in new readers and amplify the visibility of each author in the bundle.

Here's how it worked and why it's instructive:

The Campaign: "9 Killer Thrillers" Box

- What it included: Nine standalone thriller novels bundled together and sold as a single discounted ebook package.
- Goal: Reader acquisition—not immediate profit. New readers could discover multiple authors at once.
- Execution: Coordinated formatting, cover design, centralized launch date, and cross-promotion via each author's platform.

Results & Impact

- The boxed set debuted at #69 in Amazon's Top 100 overall, before resting at around #300 over the following days
- Thousands of bundles sold at $0.99–$1.99, introducing each author to a wider audience.
- Participating authors—including Blake—reported significant increases in their backlist sales and new newsletter subscribers.

- Authorship credit was shared, but each author captured long-term discovery from readers who liked one book and sought more.

Why the "Book-in-a-Box" Model Worked

Feature	Benefit
Multi-author collaboration	Cross-pollination of audiences; fans of one author received exposure to others.
Bargain pricing	Low price point encouraged impulse purchases—buyers got 9 books for the price of one.
Coordinated marketing	Shared graphics, launch timing, and calls-to-action amplified visibility on platforms like Amazon and newsletter lists.
Long-tail effects	New readers often bought additional titles individually after enjoying one in the bundle.

Tips for Authors Considering a "Book-in-a-Box" Campaign

1. Choose authors whose tone or subgenre align—don't just bundle randomly. Reader overlap is key.
2. Agree on price point strategically—keep it low enough

to attract browsers, but high enough to cover costs.

3. Prepare coordinated launch materials—shared graphics, newsletter copy, social posts.
4. Promote broadly before and after launch—each author pushes to their audience, then continues follow-up.
5. Measure long-term success—track not just bundle sales, but reader engagement and follow-on purchases.

Russell Blake's "9 Killer Thrillers" boxed set campaign stands out as one of the earliest and most effective indie thriller "book-in-a-box" launches. It provided authors with reader discovery, cross-genre exposure, algorithm boosts, and multiple streams of visibility—all while offering an irresistible value package to thriller fans.

If you're an indie author in thriller or suspense looking to break through, this model is still one of the most scalable, fun, and effective ways to introduce your work to new readers.

 ## CASE STUDY: Alexander Besher's QR T-Shirt Novel Launch

In the early 2000s, before QR codes were ubiquitous, science fiction author Alexander Besher sought an affordable, creative way to promote his novel *Manga Man* in Japan—a market where QR adoption was high but smartphone-based book marketing was novel.

The Strategy: Wear Your Book

Instead of conventional advertising, Besher printed a QR code on a T-shirt. This code linked directly to his novel's web page or mobile app, where readers could access the novel itself. By wearing the shirt in public, he turned himself into a walking billboard—a physical imprint of his digital content.

- This concept leveraged Japan's then-widespread QR code usage.
- The campaign was location-independent, low-cost, and attention-grabbing—especially in crowded urban areas like Tokyo.

Results & Learnings

- In Asia, where QR codes were widely scanned, this innovation stood out and engaged tech-savvy audiences.
- In the U.S., where QR codes were less common at the time, the method drew curiosity—even when technical barriers (like lack of scanning apps) limited deeper reach.

Lesson: Creative use of physical media + digital access can create memorable author experiences—especially when aligned with local tech habits.

And let's look at two more examples, these ones of authors creating treasure hunts that engaged readers so well that one particular treasure hunt has continued even after the author's death.

 CASE STUDY:
Jon Collins-Black — *There's Treasure Inside*

Overview

Jon Collins-Black, an entrepreneur and fantasy enthusiast, authored *There's Treasure Inside*, a book designed to lead readers on a real-world treasure hunt across the United States. He hid five treasure chests—collectively valued at over $2 million—filled with Bitcoin, historical artifacts (e.g. a glass once owned by George Washington), rare Pokémon cards, and gold. Clues to their locations are embedded in the book's pages.

Strategy & Execution

- **Clue-based treasure map:** Readers must purchase the book to access cryptic clues that guide them to chest locations.
- **Public yet private:** Chests are buried on public land, near roads, with no trespassing required—designed for safety and accessibility.
- **Value-driven urgency:** With only five chests and high-value prizes, readers are motivated to act quickly.
- **Media coverage:** Garnered mainstream attention from major outlets (e.g. Business Insider, CNN, The Guardian), generating buzz without paid ads.

Outcomes

- **Sales-boosting:** Book becomes both clue guide and collectible—a physical key to real treasure.
- **Engagement:** Readers form hunting communities around the adventure.
- **Ongoing traction:** Collins-Black promises additional clues if chests remain unfound—maintains long-term interest.

 **CASE STUDY:**
Byron Preiss — The Secret (1982)

Overview

In 1982, Byron Preiss published *The Secret,* a puzzle book that sent readers on a national treasure hunt in Canada and the U.S. Twelve small treasure boxes containing gems were buried in significant cities. Solving the book's twelve puzzles and matching illustrations to locations earned hunters the prize.

Strategy & Execution

- **Puzzle + picture:** Each clue combined text, illustration, and wordplay requiring thoughtful decoding and exploration.
- **Geographic spread:** Boxes were buried in twelve public locations across North America, hooking readers in multiple markets.
- **Redemption:** Hunters who physically retrieved a box could exchange it for a precious gemstone from Preiss.
- **Mystery legacy:** Only three of the twelve buried treasures have been found. The remaining nine continue to intrigue treasure hunters and puzzle communities.

Outcomes

- **Evergreen engagement:** Decades later, fans still search for the remaining boxes.
- **Cult following:** The Secret became a beloved reference in puzzle and treasure-hunt lore.
- **Longevity:** Despite Preiss's passing in 2005, the treasure hunt lives on as a popular mystery-solving pursuit.

Side-by-Side Comparison

Feature	Jon Collins-Black	Byron Preiss
Clue format	Novel with textual and visual clues	Picture + verse puzzle book
Prize	High-value real-world treasure chests	Precious gems for recovered boxes
Geographic scope	U.S. only	Canada & U.S. (12 cities)
Media & marketing	Press coverage & viral appeal	Word-of-mouth and puzzle community
Legacy	Ongoing hunt, evolving clues	Cult favorite, partially unsolved

 Key Takeaways for Authors

1. Create real stakes. Whether literal treasure or symbolic value, tangible reward hooks readers.
2. Make clues central to the book. Integrating puzzles or maps adds value to the reader experience.
3. Consider accessibility. Public locations and clarity in instructions reduce risk and widen participation.
4. Leverage scarcity and timing. Limited prizes and evolving clues drive urgency and sustained interest.
5. Plan for legacy. Open-ended hunts or unsolved puzzles engage readers over years or decades.

Conclusion

Both Jon Collins-Black and Byron Preiss demonstrate how treasure hunts embedded in books transcend traditional marketing. By blending narrative, location, and reward, they turned reading into an adventure, building excitement, press buzz, and lasting engagement.

Takeaways Across Case Studies

- **Creativity is key:** Memorable campaigns, whether physical or digital, stick with readers.
- **Integration matters:** Combining offline and online elements increases reach and engagement.
- **Targeted engagement pays off:** Influencers, local communities, or niche fans amplify campaigns organically.
- **Small budgets can succeed:** Guerrilla marketing leverages creativity rather than money, proving that impactful campaigns don't need massive funding.

Tips for Successful Guerrilla Marketing

1. **Know Your Audience:** Choose tactics that will resonate with your target readers.
2. Be Memorable: Aim for experiences readers will talk about.
3. **Measure Impact:** Track engagement—social media shares, newsletter sign-ups, or sales spikes.
4. **Stay Legal and Safe:** Always secure permissions for public displays or events.
5. **Blend with Other Strategies:** Guerrilla tactics work best when part of a larger marketing plan, not in isolation.

QUICK CHECKLIST:
Creative & Guerrilla Marketing

- Have I brainstormed low-cost, high-impact marketing ideas for my book?
- Are my campaigns interactive or shareable to encourage reader participation?
- Do I have a way to measure impact, even if it's social media engagement or newsletter sign-ups?
- Have I considered partnerships or collaborations to amplify reach?
- Are my ideas aligned with my book's brand and audience?

Summary

Creative and guerrilla marketing allows authors to stand out in a crowded market. From street-level campaigns and pop-up events to shareable social media challenges, these tactics are about attention, engagement, and memorability.

Even small, inventive campaigns can yield outsized results, especially when integrated with your launch plan, social media, and email marketing. The secret is creativity, authenticity, and strategic thinking—making readers part of the story, and turning your marketing into an experience rather than just an announcement.

References

- Levinson, J. C. (2007). *Guerrilla Marketing: Easy and Inexpensive Strategies for Making Big Profits from Your Small Business.* Houghton Mifflin.
- Nielsen Book Research. (2019). "Understanding Book Buyer Behavior".

CHAPTER 12
PUBLICITY AND MEDIA OUTREACH: GETTING YOUR BOOK SEEN

Even with excellent marketing, branding, and creative campaigns, nothing amplifies your reach quite like media coverage and publicity. Publicity isn't just about press releases; it's about strategically connecting your book to journalists, bloggers, podcasters, and influencers who can spread your story to thousands—or even millions—of potential readers. You can do this by hiring a publicist to represent you or you can learn how to connect with members of the media yourself.

This chapter covers how to approach media outreach, craft compelling stories, and maximize your visibility without relying solely on ads or organic reach.

Why Publicity Matters

Media coverage can:

- Reach audiences you might never access on your own.
- Lend credibility and authority to your book.
- Create a ripple effect, with articles, interviews, and features leading to social shares, reviews, and sales.

Unlike ads, publicity is often perceived as earned rather than bought, which gives it a persuasive edge in the eyes of readers.

Building Your Media List

Before you pitch anyone, you need a clear idea of who to contact:

1. Journalists & Reporters
- Focus on book reviewers, lifestyle reporters, or science/genre-specific journalists.
- Look for writers who have covered books similar to yours.
- And if your book is nonfiction or fiction and can be tied to a news peg (a topic currently being covered by media), then reach out to the reporters or journalists covering that topic. For example, when my novel *Sometimes Art Can't Save You* was released in 2005, studies that had just been released focused on the percentage of people who were self-harming. The main character in my novel is a teenager artist who self-injures (cuts) so we geared the press kit to those studies and I was offered as someone who could talk about the topic.

2. Book Bloggers and Reviewers
- Thousands of niche book bloggers actively review new titles.
- Many maintain active social media followings, amplifying coverage.

3. Podcasters and YouTube Creators
- Podcasts are growing rapidly in influence.
- Reach out to shows that align with your genre, themes, or audience demographics.

4. Local Media Outlets
- Local newspapers, radio stations, and TV shows love supporting regional authors.
- You can often get coverage with smaller, targeted pitches.

Tip: Build a spreadsheet with names, contact info, social handles, and previous coverage to organize your outreach. Include a column on the spreadsheet for when you've pitched them and their response.

Crafting Your Pitch

Your pitch is the first impression journalists or bloggers will have. A strong pitch is:

1. **Personalized:** Reference a previous article, podcast, or review they did.
2. **Concise:** Keep it short, focused, and scannable (which means smaller paragraphs with a lot of white space and headings to break up the text).
3. **Compelling:** Highlight the unique angle or hook of your book.

4. **Actionable:** Include what you're offering—review copies, interview availability, or exclusive content.

Example Pitch:

Subject: Local Author Explores Small-Town Mysteries in New Cozy Novel

Hi, [Name],

I'm Faith Walker, author of *Deadly Lies and Dog-Eared Secrets*, a cozy mystery set in Cottageville, Iowa. Your recent article on small-town fiction caught my eye, and I thought you might be interested in my book. It's a murder mystery with a lovable amateur dog-grooming sleuth and a red heeler Australian cattle dog sidekick named Whiskey, and it is perfect for readers who love animals and enjoy engaging, character-driven stories.

I'd be happy to provide a review copy, an author interview, and FAQs, plus a high resolution image of the book cover.

Thank you for your time and consideration. I look forward to your reply.

Sincerely,
Jill L. Ferguson (one half of the brother-sister writing team known as Faith Walker)
[Website] | [Social Media]

You may also want to send a whole press kit, containing a press release, FAQs, an author photo, a copy of the book, a copy of the book's front cover, and any other pertinent information to journalists. This can be sent as a physical package or as an electronic submission.

Types of Media Coverage

1. **Reviews**– Book reviews in print or online increase credibility and discoverability.
2. **Feature Articles**– Story angles, author profiles, or thematic tie-ins can introduce your book to a new audience.
3. **Interviews**– Print, podcast, or video interviews give readers a personal connection to you and your work.
4. **Guest Articles / Op-Eds**– Share your expertise, research, or insights related to your book's subject matter.
5. **Event Coverage**– Book signings, readings, or launch parties can attract local press attention.

Strategies for Successful Media Outreach

1. Timing is Key
- Start your outreach 3–6 months before launch for print features.
- For short lead-time media (blogs, podcasts), 4–6 weeks before release is sufficient.

2. Offer Exclusive Content
- Exclusive excerpts, behind-the-scenes insights, or early access to chapters increase media interest.

3. Follow Up, but Don't Spam
- A polite follow-up 1–2 weeks after the initial pitch is acceptable.
- Avoid excessive emails—journalists receive dozens daily.

4. Leverage Existing Media Relationships
- If a journalist or blogger has covered you before,

personalize outreach and highlight updates or new angles.

5. Track Your Coverage

- Keep a media tracker: outlet, type of coverage, date, and links.
- Repurpose coverage on your website, social media, and newsletters to amplify impact.

CASE STUDY COLLECTION: How Media Coverage Made Bestsellers

Part 1: Tara Westover — *Educated* (2018)

Background

Tara Westover's memoir *Educated* told the story of her survivalist childhood in Idaho and her journey to earn a PhD from Cambridge. The book had an inspiring, dramatic premise, but it was media coverage that transformed it into a global cultural phenomenon.

Media Strategy & Coverage

- Television & Radio: Appeared on *60 Minutes*, *The Daily Show*, and NPR's *Fresh Air*.
- Print Reviews: Praised by *The New York Times*, *The Atlantic*, *TIME*, and *The Washington Post*.
- Buzz Cycle: Media coverage framed her as both a courageous individual and a brilliant writer, giving her story credibility and intrigue.
- Endorsements: Media exposure caught the attention of Bill Gates and Barack Obama, whose praise amplified visibility.

Results

- 2+ years on *The New York Times* Bestseller List.
- Translated into 45+ languages.
- Listed among the best books of the year by multiple outlets.
- Sparked global conversations on education, resilience, and family estrangement.

Why It Worked

Media presented Westover's life as "a story in itself"—a human-interest angle that drew in readers who might not normally pick up a memoir. The coverage legitimized the book, created momentum, and attracted endorsements that magnified its reach.

Part 2: Delia Owens — *Where the Crawdads Sing* (2018)

Background

Delia Owens was a retired wildlife scientist with no prior fiction publications when she released her debut novel *Where the Crawdads Sing.* A story about a young girl growing up in the North Carolina marshlands, blending mystery, romance, and coming-of-age themes, it had potential—but what launched it to mega-bestseller status was its media spotlight.

Media Strategy & Coverage

- Reese's Book Club Pick: Reese Witherspoon selected the novel for her book club, ensuring instant media buzz. Reese also optioned it for a film adaptation, which gave the book cultural cachet.

- Mainstream Coverage: Featured in *The New York Times, The Atlantic, Entertainment Weekly*, and NPR. Coverage emphasized both the lush, atmospheric writing and Owens's unusual career shift from scientist to novelist.
- Word-of-Mouth Amplification: Reviews framed it as "a book everyone will be talking about," which encouraged readers to pick it up to stay part of the cultural conversation.
- Sustained Press: Media outlets revisited the book frequently after it became a long-running bestseller, giving it a second wave of coverage.

Results

- Spent over 150 weeks on *The New York Times* Bestseller List (two years at #1).
- Sold more than 18 million copies worldwide.
- Adapted into a major 2022 feature film produced by Reese Witherspoon.
- Became one of the best-selling novels of the decade.

Why It Worked

- The "Reese Witherspoon effect" provided media legitimacy and celebrity endorsement.
- Media leaned into the mystique of the author—a scientist debuting with a haunting marshland novel.
- Coverage snowballed, blending book club buzz, movie adaptation news, and sustained reviews, keeping the title in public awareness for years.

Lessons for Authors

1. Media legitimizes and multiplies visibility. A feature in a respected outlet (or a celebrity endorsement amplified by media) can transform a book's trajectory.
2. Narrative matters off the page too. Both Westover and Owens had compelling personal backstories that the media used to hook audiences.
3. Media builds momentum. The more coverage a book receives, the more likely other outlets are to join the conversation.
4. Endorsements often stem from media exposure. Book clubs, celebrities, and film producers often discover books through news coverage.
5. Sustained storytelling keeps books alive. Even after launch, media revisits success stories, ensuring books remain in the cultural spotlight.

Both Westover and Owens were traditionally published authors, but let's look at an author who self-published and the media exposure he found for himself and his series.

 CASE STUDY:
Mark Dawson — *The John Milton Series*
(Self-Published, 2013–)

Background

Mark Dawson, a British indie thriller author, self-published his *John Milton* series, often described as "James Bond meets Jason Bourne." Like many self-published authors, he struggled initially to reach readers despite strong writing. What changed the game for him was media coverage through podcasts.

Media Strategy & Coverage

- **Podcast Guesting:** Dawson began appearing on high-profile writing and publishing podcasts such as *The Creative Penn* (Joanna Penn), *The Self-Publishing Formula* (which he later co-founded), and others.
- **Transparency as Marketing:** He openly discussed his journey, marketing experiments, and even earnings, which made him a trusted voice in the indie community.
- **Education & Cross-Promotion:** Podcasts didn't just introduce him to readers but also to *thousands of aspiring writers*. By sharing his expertise, he grew a loyal audience that also bought his books.
- **Ongoing Presence:** His regular podcast appearances kept his name in circulation, functioning like long-form, evergreen ads that continued to drive new readers months or years later.

Results

- Grew his mailing list into the hundreds of thousands, many of whom discovered him through podcast interviews.
- Sold millions of copies of his thrillers worldwide, building a six-figure annual income.
- Launched *The Self-Publishing Show* podcast and educational courses, further expanding his brand and audience reach.

Why It Worked

- **Authenticity:** Hearing an author's voice and personality on a podcast built reader trust.
- **Education as Marketing:** By teaching others how

to succeed, Dawson positioned himself as both an authority and a storyteller worth following.

- **Podcast Reach:** Many podcasts live on indefinitely. A 2015 interview could still introduce him to new readers in 2025.

 ## Key Takeaways Across All Three Case Studies

1. **Media is a multiplier.** Whether through TV (Educated), celebrity-backed book clubs (Crawdads), or podcasts (Mark Dawson), exposure creates credibility and accelerates word-of-mouth.
2. **The author's story matters as much as the book's story.** Audiences connected with Westover's survivalist past, Owens's scientist-turned-novelist journey, and Dawson's indie underdog rise.
3. **Different media channels fit different authors.** Big publishers can land 60 Minutes; indie authors may find more traction on podcasts or niche blogs.
4. **Sustained presence is critical.** All three examples show how continued media attention—not just a single burst—builds long-term bestseller momentum.

Conclusion

From Tara Westover's traditional media blitz, to Delia Owens's Reese Witherspoon boost, to Mark Dawson's podcast-powered indie success, the lesson is clear: books don't just need readers, they need storytellers in the media to amplify their reach.

 ## Quick Publicity Checklist

1. Have I identified journalists, bloggers, and podcasters

relevant to my book?

2. Have I crafted personalized, compelling pitches?
3. Am I offering media outlets something unique or exclusive?
4. Have I timed outreach for optimal coverage before launch?
5. Am I tracking all coverage and repurposing it for marketing?

 ## Summary

Publicity and media outreach extend your book's reach beyond your existing audience, build credibility, and generate long-term buzz. By:

- Researching and targeting relevant media
- Crafting concise, compelling pitches
- Providing exclusive content
- Following up strategically
- Leveraging coverage across platforms

...authors can create earned exposure that amplifies all other marketing efforts.

Publicity isn't instant, but it's one of the most sustainable ways to grow visibility, credibility, and readership over time.

References:

- Nielsen Book Research. (2019). "Understanding Book Buyer Behavior."
- Bowker. (2021). "Self-Publishing and Media Outreach Trends."

Media Outreach Workflow for Authors

Media Types & Strategies

1. Book Bloggers
   - Lead time: 4–6 weeks
   - Pitch: Personalized email + ARC
   - Outcome: Reviews & social buzz
2. Journalists
   - Lead time: 3–6 months
   - Pitch: Human-interest hook or local tie-in
   - Outcome: Articles, features
3. Podcasts
   - Lead time: 4–6 weeks
   - Pitch: Exclusive interview, story behind the story
   - Outcome: Episodes, listener reach
4. YouTube Creators
   - Lead time: 4–6 weeks
   - Pitch: Visual story appeal + early access
   - Outcome: Video reviews, comments
5. Local Media
   - Lead time: 6–12 weeks
   - Pitch: Author background, events
   - Outcome: Regional awareness
6. Online Communities
   - Lead time: 2–4 weeks
   - Pitch: Share excerpt, Q&A
   - Outcome: Word-of-mouth engagement
7. Special Features
   - Lead time: 3–6 months
   - Pitch: Trend or social-topic connection
   - Outcome: Feature articles, expanded reach

Workflow Process

Identify Targets → *Craft Pitch* →
Send Pitch → *Follow-Up* → *Track &*
Repurpose Coverage → *Measure Impact*

(Loopback: to show continuous improvement)

CHAPTER 13
FROM THE PAGE TO THE STAGE: SPEAKING, TEACHING, AND EVENTS

Marketing your book isn't just about what happens online. In fact, some of the most powerful—and memorable—promotional strategies take place in person. Stepping into the world of speaking, teaching, and events allows you to become the face behind the words, build personal connections, and create buzz that lasts long after the event is over.

Whether you're leading a workshop at a library, speaking on a panel at a conference, or hosting your own launch party, events give readers a chance to engage with you as a human being, not just a name on a book cover. And here's the real secret: when people feel personally connected to an author, they're far more likely to become loyal readers and recommend your book to others (Gibson, *Book Marketing for Authors*, 2020).

Why Events Work for Authors

Events create three essential outcomes: visibility, credibility, and community.

1. **Visibility** – Events put you in front of audiences who may never have discovered your book otherwise.
2. **Credibility** – Being invited to speak positions you as an authority. Even a small workshop signals expertise.
3. **Community** – People who hear you speak and interact with you in person feel invested. They often become superfans who bring friends along for future events.

A survey from Eventbrite showed that 78% of people say they're more likely to purchase from a brand after attending an in-person event (Eventbrite, 2018). That statistic translates directly to books.

Types of Events for Authors

You don't need to limit yourself to traditional bookstore signings. There's a wide menu of possibilities, depending on your genre, audience, and personal comfort level.

1. Book Launch Parties

Think of a launch party as a birthday celebration for your book. These can be as small as a cozy gathering at your local indie bookstore or as large as a rented community hall filled with readers, music, and refreshments. Invite friends, family, press, book clubs, and local influencers. Add a signing table, reading, and Q&A for maximum engagement.

2. Library Talks

Libraries love supporting local and emerging authors. Pitch a talk or workshop related to your book's theme. For example, if you've written historical fiction, you could host a session on "Everyday Life in the Victorian Era." Nonfiction authors can easily align with education or community programs.

3. Workshops and Classes

If your book solves a problem, teaches a skill, or inspires creativity, you can expand that knowledge into workshops. Nonfiction authors often thrive here, but even novelists can create engaging classes (for example: a thriller writer leading a class on "Building Suspense in Your Writing").

4. Conferences and Festivals

Literary festivals, writing conferences, and genre-specific events (romance, mystery, sci-fi) are magnets for readers. Apply early to speak on panels, offer readings, or join signings. Conferences provide credibility, networking, and often great press coverage.

5. Virtual Events

Since 2020, virtual events have become a norm. Hosting online book launches, live Q&A sessions on Instagram or Facebook, or even a webinar series allows you to reach a global audience without leaving your desk.

Making Events Work for You

1. **Know Your Audience:** Who attends the event? Are they readers, writers, professionals, students? Tailor your talk accordingly.

2. **Offer More Than a Reading:** While a short reading can be powerful, audiences often crave interaction. Mix in stories about your writing journey, practical tips, or behind-the-scenes insights.

3. **Engage, Don't Lecture:** Ask questions, encourage discussion, and include activities where possible. Interactive sessions leave stronger impressions.

4. **Have Books on Hand:** It sounds obvious, but always arrange to have copies available. Bring a Square reader or a Venmo QR code for easy sales.

5. **Leverage Publicity:** Promote the event across your social media, website, and newsletter. Afterward, post photos, thank attendees, and share highlights.

 **SHORT CASE STUDY: Neil Gaiman's Event Magic**

Neil Gaiman is one of the most beloved modern authors, not just because of his writing, but because of his events. He doesn't just read—he performs. His live readings are full of theatrical delivery, storytelling charm, and audience interaction.

When he tours, fans line up for hours not only to buy books but to be part of the experience. Gaiman's events create lasting memories that spread by word-of-mouth and social sharing. His approach illustrates the power of bringing personality to live appearances.

Tips for Introverts

Many authors are introverts, and the idea of speaking to a

crowd can feel intimidating. Here are a few ways to ease into it:

- **Start small**—host a reading for friends at a coffee shop.
- **Partner with another author** for a joint event so you're not alone on stage.
- **Prepare and rehearse.** The more you know what you'll say, the less nervous you'll feel.
- **Remember:** the audience wants you to succeed—they're there because they already care about books.

The Long Tail of Events

Events aren't just about that one day. They create stories, photos, videos, and social proof that continue to market your book long after the chairs are put away. A single talk might spark invitations to other opportunities: podcasts, school visits, corporate gigs, or even paid speaking engagements.

Think of events as seeds you plant. Some bloom immediately in book sales; others grow slowly into bigger opportunities.

 ## Key Takeaways for Authors

Speaking, teaching, and events aren't just add-ons to your marketing strategy—they're accelerators of connection. Every handshake, every laugh during a reading, every thoughtful answer to an audience question brings readers closer to becoming fans.

References:

- Eventbrite. (2018). The 2018 *Eventbrite Pulse Report: What's happening in the events industry.* Eventbrite. https://www.eventbrite.com

- Gibson, J. (2020). *Book Marketing for Authors: Proven Strategies for Selling Your Book.* Indie Ink Press.

CHAPTER 14
BUILDING YOUR AUTHOR BUSINESS

So, you've published a book (or you're planning to). You've done the pre-launch hustle, crafted a marketing plan, maybe even scored a few glowing reviews or local TV spots. First off—congratulations! That's no small feat. But here's the thing: writing and marketing your first book isn't the finish line. It's the starting line of a much bigger, richer journey: building your author business.

If you want to build a sustainable career as an author, it's time to think like an entrepreneur. Whether your dream is to write full-time or to create a thriving side hustle alongside another career, treating your writing as a business—rather than a one-time creative project—will make the difference between a passion project and a profitable path.

This chapter will walk you through how to create, grow, and sustain your author business. We'll cover the mindset shifts you need to make, practical steps for structuring your business, how to manage multiple income streams, and how to build the systems that support long-term success. Think of this as your roadmap to moving from "someone who wrote a book" to "someone running a book-based business."

1. The Mindset Shift: From Writer to Authorpreneur

The first hurdle is often mental. Many writers see themselves solely as creatives, reluctant to think about "business stuff." But if you want your books to pay the bills—or even just reliably cover your coffee and laptop upgrades—you need to embrace the idea of being both an artist and an entrepreneur.

The hybrid term "authorpreneur" has gained popularity because it captures this dual identity. As Joanna Penn, a bestselling indie author and founder of *The Creative Penn*, puts it: "Being an author is no longer just about writing. It's about understanding business, marketing, branding, and the long game of creating intellectual property that can earn you money for years to come." (Penn, *Business for Authors*, 2014)

Why This Matters:

- **Sustainability:** A business mindset encourages long-term planning, so you're not relying solely on the unpredictable spikes of book launches.
- **Multiple Income Streams:** You start thinking beyond book sales into speaking, courses, audiobooks, and more.
- **Control:** You stop waiting for publishers, bookstores,

or luck, and instead create proactive strategies to reach readers.

2. Laying the Foundation: Structuring Your Author Business

Just as you wouldn't build a house without a foundation, you can't build a lasting author business without some structure. Here's what to consider:

A. Decide on a Legal Structure
- **Sole Proprietor:** Easiest for beginners; you and your business are legally the same entity.
- **LLC (Limited Liability Company):** Offers protection of personal assets and may bring tax advantages.
- **Corporation (S-Corp, C-Corp):** Usually only necessary at higher income levels or for authors running larger-scale publishing enterprises. (You can read about these a bit more in depth in my book *Creating a Freelance Career*) published by Routledge.

Tip: Start simple. Many authors begin as sole proprietors and upgrade to LLCs once their income grows.

B. Get Your Finances in Order
- Open a separate business bank account to keep book income and expenses apart from personal money.
- Consider using accounting software like QuickBooks, Wave, or FreshBooks.
- Track everything: ISBNs, cover design costs, editing fees, ads, conference registrations—all of it is tax-deductible.

C. Build Your "Author HQ"
Think of this as your digital storefront:

- A professional website (ideally yourname.com).
- A strong email list (via MailerLite, ConvertKit, etc.).
- Social media channels that fit your personality and audience.

These aren't just marketing tools; they're the infrastructure of your business.

3. Revenue Streams: Beyond Book Sales

Here's the truth most authors don't want to hear: book royalties alone often aren't enough to make a sustainable living. According to a 2019 Authors Guild survey, median income for full-time authors was about $20,300/year from books alone (Authors Guild, 2019). That's sobering—but here's the good news: you can stack multiple streams of income to build a much healthier business.

Primary Income Streams for Authors

1. Book Sales
- **Print** (paperback, hardcover, print-on-demand).
- **Ebooks** (Amazon Kindle, Apple Books, Kobo, Google Play).
- **Audiobooks** (Audible, Findaway Voices or Authors Republic).

2. Public Speaking & Events
- Paid keynote speeches.
- Library talks, school visits.
- Literary festivals and conferences.

3. Teaching & Workshops
- Online courses (Teachable, Thinkific).
- Masterclasses or webinars.
- Writing retreats.

4. Freelance Opportunities
- Ghostwriting, editing, coaching.
- Journalism or content writing.

5. Merchandise & Licensing
- Book-themed merchandise (mugs, T-shirts, tote bags).
- Licensing characters or settings for games/film.

6. Patronage & Crowdfunding
- Patreon, Ko-fi, or Kickstarter campaigns for special projects.

7. Affiliate & Partnership Marketing
- Earning commissions by recommending tools, books, or services.

Think Like an Investor

Each book you write is like an asset—an intellectual property (IP) that can earn in multiple formats, across multiple platforms, for decades.

Case in point: J.K. Rowling doesn't just make money from *Harry Potter* book sales. The IP spawned films, games, theme parks, merchandise, and licensing deals. Obviously, not every author will reach that scale, but the principle applies: one story, many formats.

4. Branding: You Are the Business

Your author brand is not just your logo or your website colors—it's the perception readers have of you

Ask yourself:

- What genre do I write in?
- What emotions do I want readers to associate with my work?
- What kind of community do I want to build?

For example:

- Colleen Hoover built her brand on emotionally intense, romantic stories and now has an army of loyal "CoHorts."
- Neil Gaiman brands himself as a multi-genre storyteller who brings magic and mythology into everyday life.

Your brand helps readers know what to expect and makes you recognizable in a crowded market.

5. Systems and Productivity: Treating Your Writing Like Work

If you're serious about your author business, you need systems. Systems keep you consistent, reduce stress, and help you scale.

Writing Systems
- Set a production schedule (word count goals, publishing timeline).
- Use tools like Scrivener, Notion, or Trello to organize projects.

Marketing Systems
- Batch-create social media posts.
- Automate email sequences (welcome emails, launch campaigns).
- Use scheduling tools like Buffer or Later.

Administrative Systems
- Create standard contracts for speaking gigs or freelance work.
- Use templates for pitch emails.
- Block time monthly for finances and tax prep.

Remember: systems don't limit creativity—they free up brain space for it.

6. Scaling: From One Book to a Body of Work

If you want to build a career, not just launch a single book, the next step is scaling.

A. Write the Next Book
One of the best marketing strategies is always: write more books. A series or a backlist multiplies your income and reader loyalty.

B. Create Spin-Off Products
- Bundle ebooks into box sets.
- Release special editions (signed hardcovers, annotated versions).
- Expand into companion guides or workbooks.

C. Repurpose Content
- Turn a book into an online course.
- Adapt short stories into podcasts.

- Share excerpts as blog posts or newsletters.

7. Networking and Partnerships

No author is an island. Building relationships is critical for growth.

- **Other Authors:** Cross-promote, co-host events, join anthologies.
- **Bookstores & Libraries:** Local support builds grassroots sales.
- **Influencers & Bloggers:** Reach new audiences through reviews and features.
- **Industry Professionals:** Editors, designers, publicists—treat them as partners, not just vendors.

Partnerships expand your reach exponentially compared to going solo.

8. Longevity: Thinking Decades Ahead

A true author business isn't built on one launch or one viral moment. It's built on consistency, adaptability, and resilience.

- **Rights Management:** Keep track of your contracts—film rights, translation rights, audio rights. Each is a potential future payday.
- **Retirement & Royalties:** Consider that royalties can act like a pension, generating passive income even when you're no longer writing actively.
- **Future-Proofing:** Stay adaptable as technology changes (remember when ebooks first disrupted the industry?).

The key is to think of your career as a marathon, not a sprint.

CASE STUDY:
Joanna Penn – From Writer to Author Entrepreneur

Joanna Penn is one of the most well-known examples of how an author can turn writing into a thriving, multi-faceted business. She began her journey like many writers: with one book, self-published in 2008. That book, a nonfiction title called *How to Enjoy Your Job... Or Find a New One*, didn't set the world on fire. In fact, she has admitted that sales were disappointing. But instead of giving up, Penn treated the experience as a crash course in publishing and marketing. That mindset shift—viewing each book not as a one-off product but as a stepping stone in a long-term business—became the cornerstone of her success.

Early Lessons and Rebranding

Joanna quickly realized that her first book's struggles weren't because she was a bad writer, but because she lacked a brand, an audience, and a clear long-term plan. She rebranded herself as "The Creative Penn," a name that would later become synonymous with practical publishing advice. She started blogging in 2008 about writing, marketing, and publishing, not only to share what she was learning but also to attract an audience of like-minded writers and readers.

Her blog laid the foundation for her mailing list, which grew steadily over time. It also positioned her as a credible voice in the emerging world of indie publishing, even before self-publishing had gained mainstream respectability.

Building Multiple Income Streams

Penn realized early that relying solely on book sales was risky. Instead, she focused on building multiple income streams, a hallmark of any serious business. Today, her author business includes:

1. **Fiction and Nonfiction Books** – She writes thrillers under J.F. Penn and nonfiction under Joanna Penn. This diversification allows her to reach different markets.
2. **Podcasting** – *The Creative Penn Podcast*, launched in 2009, has become one of the most respected shows on writing and publishing, bringing in sponsorship income and strengthening her brand authority.
3. **Courses and Workshops** – Penn sells digital courses on topics like self-publishing, marketing, and creative business. These not only provide income but also deepen her authority as a teacher.
4. **Affiliate Income** – By recommending tools and services she uses, Joanna earns commission income. This is often overlooked by authors but can add up to a significant stream.
5. **Speaking Engagements** – She speaks internationally at writing conferences, both paid and as a way to promote her books.
6. **Consulting and Services** – While not her main focus anymore, in the early days she offered consulting, which gave her insights into authors' needs.

By 2015, Penn reported that her author business had grown into a six-figure operation. In subsequent years, she has continued to refine her strategy and evolve alongside industry trends.

Treating Writing as Intellectual Property

One of Penn's key business philosophies is that books are not just "products"—they are intellectual property assets. Each book has the potential to generate revenue in multiple ways: e-books, paperbacks, audiobooks, translations, special editions, licensing, and more. She emphasizes thinking beyond a single format or release.

For example, her thriller novels have been translated into multiple languages, and her nonfiction is available in audio formats narrated by her and other professionals. This multiplies her income without requiring her to write new content every time.

Leveraging Global Reach

Penn has always taken a global approach to publishing. Instead of focusing solely on the U.S. or U.K. markets, she embraced platforms like Kobo, Apple Books, and Draft2Digital, which distribute worldwide. She also consistently advocates for "going wide" instead of relying exclusively on Amazon. By doing so, she future-proofed her business against changes in one retailer's policies.

Scaling Through Systems

As her business grew, Penn implemented systems to manage it sustainably. She automated parts of her marketing (email sequences, evergreen blog content, podcast distribution), hired contractors for tasks like cover design and editing, and developed a repeatable process for book launches. This shift from a "do-everything-yourself" mindset to a "delegate and systemize" approach is what allowed her to scale.

Mindset and Longevity

Joanna Penn is also vocal about the mindset required to sustain a creative business. She often speaks about the need to balance the creative drive (writing what you love) with the business perspective (understanding what readers want). She has written extensively about "surfing the change" in publishing—being adaptable as new technologies and opportunities emerge, from AI tools to subscription models.

Her emphasis on longevity is also important. She doesn't chase quick wins or viral hits. Instead, she focuses on consistent creation, building assets that pay off over time. She refers to this as the "long game" of publishing, which is one reason she remains a respected and sustainable voice in the author community more than a decade later.

 ## Key Lessons from Joanna Penn's Author Business

1. **Start before you're ready** – Her first book wasn't a hit, but it gave her the foundation to build a brand.
2. **Diversify income streams** – Don't rely on a single book or format. Spread risk and opportunity.
3. **Think globally and long-term** – Don't limit yourself to one country or short-term sales goals.
4. **Build systems and delegate** – A true business requires processes that don't depend on you doing everything.
5. **Embrace change** – From print to digital to AI, adaptability is a competitive advantage.

Key Takeaway

Joanna Penn's success is not the result of one blockbuster

book, but of building a sustainable author ecosystem. She has shown that by thinking like an entrepreneur, an author can not only make a living but create a thriving, resilient business.

Action Steps: Building Your Author Business

1. **Mindset:** Decide if you're ready to be an authorpreneur.
2. **Structure:** Choose a legal setup, separate finances, and build your author HQ.
3. **Income:** Identify 2–3 revenue streams to pursue in addition to book sales.
4. **Branding:** Define your author identity and audience.
5. **Systems:** Implement tools to manage writing, marketing, and admin.
6. **Scaling:** Plan for your next book or spin-off product.
7. **Networking:** Start cultivating meaningful partnerships.
8. **Longevity:** Think of your author career as a decades-long journey.

Final Thoughts

Building an author business is about marrying creativity with strategy. It's about playing the long game: creating a body of work, cultivating an audience, and diversifying income so you're not at the mercy of Amazon's algorithms or fleeting trends.

At the end of the day, your words are valuable. They can inspire, entertain, heal, or provoke thought—and they can also form the foundation of a thriving business if you treat them as such.

So, take a deep breath, grab your notebook (or spreadsheet), and start laying the bricks of your author empire.

Let's look at one more case study of an author who has certainly become an authorpreneur, churning out new books every five weeks.

 ## CASE STUDY:
Addison Moore – Building a Career Through Indie Publishing and Reader Connection

The Context: Breaking into a Crowded Market

When Addison Moore entered the self-publishing scene in the early 2010s, the digital landscape was exploding. The Kindle revolution had lowered barriers for independent authors, but it also meant the market was flooded with content. Standing out required not only writing skill but also sharp marketing instincts and a deep understanding of reader behavior.

Moore, who writes primarily young adult paranormal romance and contemporary romance, as well as cozy mysteries, tapped into two key trends:

1. The rising popularity of paranormal romance following *Twilight* (Stephanie Meyer) and *The Vampire Diaries.*
2. The binge-reading habits of romance readers, who prefer series that keep them hooked.

Her breakout series, *Celestra,* perfectly aligned with these reader desires.

Strategy 1: Writing in High-Demand Genres

Moore understood that YA and romance readers, as well as mystery readers, are voracious consumers who love multi-book series. By writing a paranormal romance that mixed elements of fantasy, forbidden love, and high school drama, she positioned her books in a commercial sweet spot.

She also expanded into contemporary romance with series like *3:AM Kisses*, recognizing that romance readers often cross between subgenres and enjoy both fantasy escapism and real-world love stories. This diversification allowed her to grow her audience without alienating her core fans.

Lesson: Know your readers' reading habits—if they love series, give them more books to binge.

Strategy 2: Leveraging Amazon's Ecosystem

From early on, Moore leaned into Amazon's platform benefits. She:

- **Optimized Metadata & Keywords:** Choosing smart keywords and categories helped her books appear in searches where readers were already looking.
- **Price Promotions:** She used free and 99¢ deals strategically to get her first-in-series novels into as many hands as possible.
- **Rapid Release Strategy:** She understood the importance of not letting readers wait too long between books. By releasing frequently, she fed binge-readers who wanted instant gratification.

This kept her books consistently visible in Amazon rankings and built strong algorithmic momentum.

Lesson: The Amazon ecosystem rewards consistency, smart keywords, and reader-centered pricing strategies.

Strategy 3: Building Relationships with Readers

Moore has always prioritized direct reader engagement.

- She actively connects with fans on social media (particularly Facebook and Instagram), offering behind-the-scenes peeks, teasers, and casual conversations.
- She uses newsletters effectively, sending out new release updates, giveaways, and personal notes to maintain relationships beyond social media. (Though in my humble opinion, the frequency of almost daily newsletters is too often for the readers.)
- She encourages reader participation, letting fans feel like insiders in her creative process.

By creating authentic connections, she has fostered a loyal readership who eagerly awaits each new release.

Lesson: Readers who feel personally connected to an author are more likely to become repeat buyers and advocates.

Strategy 4: Branding Through Volume and Consistency

Moore's marketing strategy isn't just about one book—it's about brand recognition.

- Her covers are genre-appropriate and consistent, signaling immediately whether a series is YA paranormal or adult romance or cozy, paranormal mystery.
- She publishes prolifically, ensuring her name is always present in the market.
- She capitalizes on the power of series, with interconnected books that encourage binge reading and strong emotional investment.

By treating her author career like a brand, she positioned herself not just as a one-hit wonder but as a go-to writer in her niches.

Results: A Self-Publishing Success Story

- The *Celestra* series sold hundreds of thousands of copies, propelling her into the spotlight.
- She became a *USA Today* bestselling author, proving that indie writers could reach mass-market recognition.
- She built a sustainable, full-time career from her writing, independent of traditional publishing.

Her success has inspired countless other indie authors who now see that understanding your readers, leveraging platforms strategically, and publishing consistently can build a thriving author business.

 **Key Takeaways for Authors**

1. Write for a hungry market. Understanding what genres readers binge can give you a competitive edge.
2. Use Amazon to your advantage. Keywords, categories, and rapid releases feed the algorithm and keep you visible.
3. Engage personally. Readers want to know the author behind the book. Build community, not just an audience.
4. Think like a brand. Covers, tone, and consistency help readers instantly recognize and trust your books.

Reference:

- Penn, J. (2014). *Business for Authors: How to Be an Author Entrepreneur.* Curl Up Press.

CHAPTER 15
INDIE PUBLISHING STRATEGIES: THRIVING OUTSIDE THE TRADITIONAL PATH

I'm frequently asked by my book coaching clients if they should self-publish, hybrid publish, or try to find an agent and go the traditional publishing path. The answer to that question depends on so many factors: their goals for writing the book in the first place, what kind of and the size of their network, the type of book they are working on, how much creative control they want over the project and the entire process, how good they are at promoting themselves and products, and so much more. For some projects and people, indie publishing or self-publishing makes the most sense.

Why Indie Publishing?

A decade ago, self-publishing carried a stigma: many assumed it meant "not good enough for traditional publishing." Today, that couldn't be further from the truth. Indie publishing is now a legitimate, thriving, billion-dollar industry. In fact, according to Bowker, more than 1.7 million self-published books are released annually in the U.S. alone (Bowker, 2022).

For many authors, indie publishing offers:

- Creative control over covers, titles, and content.
- Higher royalties (up to 70% on e-books compared to 8–15% traditionally).
- Speed to market, sometimes weeks instead of years.
- Direct reader connection, without middlemen.

But with great power comes great responsibility—you're the writer, publisher, and business strategist rolled into one. In this chapter, we'll walk through the most effective indie publishing strategies to not just publish, but succeed.

1. Know Your Why
Before diving into platforms and marketing tactics, start with your purpose. Indie publishing can serve different goals:

- Do you want a career as a full-time author?
- Are you looking for side income?
- Is your book a passion project or legacy piece?

Your "why" shapes your strategy. For example, a career author may prioritize building a long-running series, while a legacy author might focus on a single high-quality book with professional editing and design.

2. Choose the Right Platforms

The indie publishing landscape is multi-platform, but where you publish determines your reach and royalties.

The Big Players:

- Amazon Kindle Direct Publishing (KDP): Dominates the e-book market (estimates suggest 60–70% market share). Offers Kindle Unlimited (KU), which pays authors based on page reads.
- IngramSpark: Best for wide distribution of print books—bookstores and libraries often order from Ingram.
- Draft2Digital (D2D): A user-friendly aggregator that distributes to Apple Books, Kobo, Barnes & Noble, and more.
- Smashwords (acquired by D2D): Still relevant for niche distribution.
- ACX (Audiobook Creation Exchange): Owned by Amazon, key for audiobook distribution on Audible. But also Authors Republic for distribution to Audible and other audio book platforms.

Strategy Decision Point:

- Exclusive with Amazon (KDP Select/KU): Great for authors targeting binge readers, especially in romance, sci-fi, and thrillers. KU often boosts visibility, but it limits distribution.
- Wide Distribution: Best for those wanting to reach global markets, libraries, and non-Amazon retailers. More resilient long-term but requires stronger marketing.

3. Professional Presentation is Non-Negotiable

Indie publishing doesn't mean DIY everything. Successful indie authors invest in:

- **Professional Editing** (developmental + copyediting + proofreading). Readers forgive a lot, but not sloppy writing.
- **Cover Design:** Covers are marketing tools, not just art. A romance cover needs to scream "romance." A thriller cover should scream "thriller." Readers judge books in seconds.
- **Formatting:** Use tools like Vellum, Atticus, or Reedsy for professional e-book and print layouts. Or hire a professional book designer who works in InDesign or a similar program to ensure your series of books has all of the same design elements. Professional designers can easily turn design files into print book interiors and epubs.

Pro Tip: Your cover isn't about "what's in your head"—it's about "what sells in your genre." Study the top 20 bestsellers in your category.

4. Series and Rapid Release Strategies

One of the strongest indie advantages is the ability to publish quickly. Traditional publishers may release one book every 1–2 years. Indie authors can release multiple per year, even per quarter.

- **Series Sell:** Romance, fantasy, mystery, and sci-fi thrive on binge readers. Each book is a funnel to the next.
- **Rapid Release:** Launching books in quick succession (e.g., every 30–90 days) keeps momentum and fuels algorithms.
- **Boxed Sets:** Great for value-seeking readers and promotions.

5. Pricing and Promotions

Unlike traditional publishers, indie authors control their pricing.

Smart Pricing Strategies:

- **Intro Pricing:** Launch a new ebook at 99¢–$2.99 to encourage downloads and reviews.
- **First-in-Series Free:** A powerful funnel tactic. Make Book 1 free, then profit on later books. Or to do this when you are marketing your blacklist.
- **Price Pulldowns:** Temporary discounts to run promotions on sites like BookBub, Freebooksy, or Robin Reads.

Promotional Sites:
- **BookBub Featured Deals:** Expensive but powerful, with massive reach.
- **Smaller Sites:** BargainBooksy, ENT (Ereader News Today), Book Cave, etc.
- **Amazon Ads:** Pay-per-click advertising within the Kindle ecosystem.
- **Facebook/Meta Ads:** Useful for building email lists and retargeting readers.

6. The Power of the Algorithm

Amazon (and other platforms) reward visibility and engagement. Your job is to feed the algorithm:

- Early reviews = credibility boost.
- Consistent sales = higher rankings.
- KU page reads = algorithm love.

Pro Tip: Think of Amazon as your biggest bookseller, not your publisher. Treat it like a partner you must constantly "feed."

7. Building a Reader Funnel

Indie publishing success isn't about one book—it's about building a long-term reader pipeline.

Funnel Example:

1. **Discoverability:** Reader finds you via ads, freebie, or recommendation.
2. **Low-Risk Entry:** Free/cheap first book.
3. **Engagement:** Reader signs up for your email list (via bonus content or exclusive story).
4. **Conversion:** Reader buys your next books or box set.
5. **Loyalty:** Reader becomes a fan, leaves reviews, and recommends you.

This funnel approach is why indie authors emphasize email lists—it's the one asset you own.

8. Marketing Beyond Amazon

Indie authors can't rely solely on "publish and pray." Marketing matters.

- **Email Lists:** Services like MailerLite or ConvertKit help you nurture readers directly.
- **Social Media:** TikTok (BookTok), Instagram, Facebook Groups. Pick one platform you enjoy and show up authentically.
- **ARC Teams:** Advanced Reader Copy groups give you early reviews and buzz.
- **Street Teams:** Loyal fans who help share your releases.

Indie authors who treat their readers like a community thrive far more than those who treat them like faceless customers.

9. Audiobooks and Beyond

The audiobook market is booming (projected to hit $19 billion globally by 2030, according to Grand View Research). Indie authors can:

- Self-produce through ACX or Findaway Voices.
- Choose between revenue share with narrators or paying upfront.
- Experiment with AI narration (emerging but controversial and still has a long ways to go for fiction).

Merchandise, Patreon exclusives, and special editions (e.g., hardcovers via Kickstarter) are also growing revenue streams.

 ## CASE STUDY:
The Indie Success of Amanda Hocking

No indie strategy chapter is complete without Amanda Hocking.

In 2010, Hocking was a struggling writer with a dozen paranormal romance manuscripts. She self-published her first titles on Kindle at $0.99–$2.99.

- Within six months, she sold over 100,000 copies.
- By 2011, she had sold over a million copies and earned more than 2 million.
- Her success was fueled by low pricing, engaging covers, and tapping into YA paranormal trends.

Hocking eventually signed with a traditional publisher but remains an icon of the indie-first revolution.

Key Lessons from Hocking:

- Low entry pricing can fuel rapid adoption.
- Hitting the right genre at the right time matters.
- Indie authors can create opportunities big enough that publishers come knocking.

11. Challenges of Indie Publishing

It's not all sunshine and royalties. Challenges include:

- **Upfront Costs:** Editing, cover design, ads—successful indies often invest $500–$5,000 per book.
- **Marketing Overwhelm:** Authors must juggle writing and promotion.
- **Market Saturation:** Millions of books compete for attention.
- **Burnout:** Rapid release pressure can take a toll.

The most successful indie authors treat their work like a business and develop sustainable systems...as I said in the previous chapter.

12. The Future of Indie Publishing

- **AI Tools:** From writing assistance and editing to narration, AI is changing the industry.
- **Subscription Models:** Kindle Unlimited, Scribd, and others shift how readers consume books.
- **Global Markets:** Growth in India, Africa, and Latin America opens new opportunities.
- **Hybrid Models:** Many authors choose a mix—self-publishing some books, traditionally publishing others.

CASE STUDY:
Hugh Howey (*Wool* and Sci-Fi Domination)

Hugh Howey's path is often cited as the sci-fi indie dream story.

- In 2011, he self-published a short dystopian story called *Wool* on Kindle.
- Reader enthusiasm drove him to expand it into a series. Word-of-mouth took off.
- By 2012, *Wool* sold hundreds of thousands of copies and caught Hollywood's attention.
- He famously retained digital rights while selling print rights to Simon & Schuster and film rights to 20th Century Fox.

Why He Stands Out:

- He proved that indie authors can negotiate hybrid deals on their own terms.
- His success highlighted the power of serialized storytelling in digital markets.
- *Wool* went on to inspire the Apple TV+ series *Silo*, showing how indie fiction can cross into mainstream media.

Key Lessons from Howey:

- Don't underestimate the potential of a novella or short story.
- Retaining rights (digital, print, film) gives indies leverage.
- Sci-fi and fantasy fans thrive in digital-first spaces.

CASE STUDY:
Bella Andre (Romance Powerhouse)

Bella Andre is often called the "queen of indie romance."

- After receiving multiple rejections from traditional publishers, she self-published her *Sullivan Series* in 2010.
- By 2012, she had sold over 2 million self-published books.
- She built a direct fanbase by releasing multiple books per year, each focused on a different member of the Sullivan family.
- In 2013, she signed a seven-figure deal with Harlequin/MIRA for print rights—while keeping her e-book rights.

Why She Stands Out:

- She mastered the rapid release strategy, giving readers a steady stream of romance stories.
- She branded her series so fans knew exactly what to expect.
- She showed that indie romance authors can compete with, and even outsell, traditional publishers.

Key Lessons from Andre:

- Romance readers are binge readers—feed them quickly.
- Owning your e-book rights ensures long-term income, even with traditional deals.
- Consistency and branding make series unforgettable.

 **Key Takeaways**

- Indie publishing isn't just about writing—it's about running a small business.
- Invest in professional presentation (editing, covers, formatting).
- Decide early: exclusive with Amazon or wide distribution.
- Build a reader funnel—email lists and series matter more than one book.
- Marketing isn't optional—it's the engine that drives visibility.
- Indie authors who embrace creativity, persistence, and business thinking can thrive.

Indie Publishing Playbook Checklist

Phase 1: Pre-Writing & Market Prep

☐ Identify Your Audience – Define your ideal reader (age, interests, genre preferences).
☐ Study the Market – Research successful titles in your genre. What tropes and covers are trending?
☐ Plan Your Series Strategy– Decide if your book will be standalone or part of a series (series sell better for indies).
☐ Outline a Release Schedule – Consider rapid-release timing to keep momentum.

Phase 2: Writing & Editing

☐ Write with Reader Expectations in Mind– Balance originality with popular tropes.
☐ Hire a Professional Editor – Developmental, copy, and/or line editing (don't skip this).

☐ Beta Readers / ARC Team – Gather early feedback from trusted readers.

☐ Polish Until Publication-Ready – Proofread multiple times (consider a professional proofreader).

Phase 3: Production & Packaging

☐ Hire a Cover Designer – Covers sell books; invest in a genre-appropriate design.

☐ Format the Book– Professionally for both ebook and print (tools: Vellum, Atticus, Draft2Digital).

☐ Write a Killer Book Description – Hook readers with emotional, benefit-driven copy.

☐ Select Metadata Smartly – Keywords, categories, and BISAC codes that boost discoverability.

☐ Secure ISBNs– Buy your own for long-term publishing control (or use platform-provided).

Phase 4: Publishing & Distribution

☐ Choose Your Platforms:
- Amazon KDP (ebook + print)
- Kindle Unlimited (exclusive) or go wide (IngramSpark, Kobo, Apple, B&N, Draft2Digital).

☐ Set Competitive Pricing – Research comparable indie and trad-pub titles.

☐ Upload with Clean Metadata – Double-check formatting, keywords, and series info.

Phase 5: Marketing & Launch

☐ Build a Launch Team – Gather superfans, beta readers, and influencers for early reviews.

☐ Schedule Promotions – Plan free days, 99¢ deals, or

newsletter promotions (BookBub, Freebooksy, Ereader News Today).

☐ Run Ads Smartly – Test Amazon Ads, Facebook Ads, or BookBub Ads with small budgets first.

☐ Engage with Readers – Send newsletters, post on social media, host launch events.

☐ Encourage Reviews – Early reviews drive sales and algorithm boosts.

Phase 6: Post-Launch & Growth

☐ Track Sales Data – Study what's working (ads, promos, pricing).

☐ Adjust Marketing Strategy – Double down on what converts, cut what doesn't.

☐ Release Frequently – Feed your readers with consistent content (novels, novellas, short stories).

☐ Build Your Backlist – A larger catalog increases visibility and income stability.

☐ Foster a Reader Community – Newsletter, reader group, or Patreon for superfans.

The Indie Author Success Formula

Right Book + Right Package + Right Audience + Consistency = Long-Term Career Growth

CHAPTER 16
YOUR STORY, YOUR LEGACY

Books are more than words on a page. They are bridges between people, ideas, and generations. As you've seen throughout this book, authors—whether indie pioneers, bestselling legends, or quiet wordsmiths finding their first readers—have all proven that publishing is no longer a gate-kept dream. It is a calling that, with creativity, persistence, and courage, you can answer.

We've traveled together through the world of building readerships, experimenting with marketing, engaging communities, testing indie publishing strategies, harnessing media, speaking on stages, and transforming passion into a sustainable business. We've examined the bold risks that paid off—Mark Dawson diving into uncharted Facebook ads, Angie Thomas transforming personal truth into cultural resonance, and countless others who refused to wait for permission.

The lesson in every case study and strategy is clear: success does not come from copying someone else's path. It comes from showing up as yourself, consistently, authentically, and courageously.

The Author's Mindset

Before you put the final touches on your book launch plan—or submit your first manuscript—pause for a moment. Remember:

- You are not "just" selling books. You are inviting readers into a story only you could write.
- You are not "just" learning marketing. You are building connections—with communities, with advocates, with future friends who haven't met you yet.
- You are not "just" an author. You are an entrepreneur, a cultural contributor, and a storyteller shaping worlds.

The most successful authors think beyond one book. They think in terms of careers, communities, and legacies. They see each launch as a stepping stone, each reader as a relationship, and each word as part of a larger conversation.

Looking Back, Looking Ahead

The publishing industry is more open and dynamic than at any other time in history. Technology has lowered barriers, readers are hungrier for connection, and the tools for reaching them have never been more accessible. Whether through Digital Ads and Analytics, Community and Authenticity, Guerrilla Creativity, or Business Acumen and Long-Term Strategy—you now have an entire playbook at your fingertips.

But knowledge alone is not enough. The authors who succeed are those who act.

Your Call to Action

So here is your charge as you close this book:

1. Choose Courage Over Fear.
Don't wait for the perfect plan. Don't wait for permission. Begin today—whether that means drafting your launch email, posting on social media, or reaching out to a book club.

2. Build Relationships, Not Just Sales.
Readers remember how you make them feel more than how many ads they see. Focus on connection.

3. Experiment Relentlessly.
Not every strategy will work for you. Some ads will flop. Some pitches will be ignored. That's not failure—it's information. Learn, adapt, and keep going.

4. Think Like a Creator and a CEO.
Your words are your art, but your career is your business. Treat it with intention, and it will sustain you for years to come.

5. Leave Your Legacy.
Every book you release is a ripple in the world. You cannot predict how far it will travel or whose life it will touch—but it will.

The Final Word

The road ahead will not always be easy. There will be rejections, slow months, and moments of doubt. But there will also be letters from readers who say your words changed them. There will be laughter at book clubs, inspiration at events, and a sense of awe when you realize that your imagination has found a permanent home in the minds of strangers.

So go forth.
Write bravely.
Market boldly.
Publish unapologetically.
Share your story with the world.

Because the truth is this: someone out there needs your book. They just don't know it yet. It's your job to make sure they find it. And they will.

Your story matters. Your voice matters. The world is waiting—turn the page and begin.

APPENDIX 1

Sample Book Marketing Plan

Book Title (Placeholder): Whispers in the Pines
Genre: Cozy Mystery
Target Audience: Adults 25–65, primarily women, fans of small-town mysteries, book clubs, and pet lovers
Launch Date: October 15, 2026

Goals

1. Sell 5,000+ copies in the first six months.
2. Build an engaged newsletter audience of 3,000+ readers.
3. Secure at least 20 media mentions (podcasts, blogs, or local press).
4. Gain traction with book clubs and cozy mystery Facebook groups.

Target Audience Profile

- Demographics: Women 30–65, U.S., U.K., and Canada, middle-income, college-educated.
- Psychographics: Enjoy cozy entertainment, pet

ownership, community values, lighthearted mysteries.
- Comparable Authors: Ellery Adams, Joanne Fluke, V.M. Burns.

Timeline

3–6 Months Before Launch

- Finalize book cover and blurb.
- Create ARC (Advance Reader Copy) files (ePub, PDF).
- Launch website and newsletter opt-in with free prequel short story.
- Start cover reveal campaign** on Instagram, TikTok, Facebook, and via newsletter.
- Apply for BookBub New Release Alert and schedule blog tours with cozy mystery bloggers.
- Research and pitch local bookstores and libraries for launch events.
- Build book club kit (discussion questions, recipes, trivia).

1–2 Months Before Launch

- Send ARCs to bookstagrammers, cozy mystery bloggers, and NetGalley (if budget allows).
- Pitch local media outlets: small-town papers, radio shows, podcasts.
- Create audiogram snippets (narrator readings of first chapter) to post on TikTok/Instagram.
- Set up Goodreads giveaway to boost early awareness.
- Begin running Facebook/Instagram ads targeting cozy mystery readers, using newsletter sign-ups as the funnel.

Launch Month

- Host virtual launch party on Facebook or Instagram Live with giveaways, Q&A, and fun trivia.
- Appear on at least 5 podcasts focused on writing, books, or cozy living.
- Schedule in-person bookstore/library signings (if available).
- Share daily social media content: behind-the-scenes posts, pet pictures (if dog/cat featured in book), reader shout-outs.
- Encourage ARC readers and launch team to post reviews on Amazon and Goodreads.
- Offer limited-time launch discount (e.g., $2.99 eBook for first week).

1–3 Months After Launch

- Run BookBub Featured Deal (if accepted) or Fussy Librarian promotion.
- Send book club outreach email with free Zoom Q&A offer.
- Continue social media ads (retargeting website visitors and newsletter subscribers).
- Pitch guest blog posts to cozy lifestyle or pet-friendly websites.
- Release a bonus short story (newsletter exclusive) to keep readers engaged.

Long-Term (6–12 Months After Launch)

- Cross-promote with other cozy mystery authors (newsletter swaps, joint giveaways).
- Package book into a boxed set or KU promotion if in a

series.

- Pitch book for library reading groups and cozy mystery conventions.
- Continue building reader community through Facebook group or Patreon.
- Work on the next book in the series and begin pre-launch marketing early.

Marketing Tactics

Digital Marketing

- Social Media: Instagram Reels & TikTok for fun "cozy mystery + pet" content.
- Email Marketing: Weekly updates, behind-the-scenes content, exclusive goodies.
- Amazon Ads: Target readers of similar cozy authors.
- Facebook Ads: Lead generation for newsletter + launch announcement campaigns.

Publicity & Media

- Local newspapers, radio, podcasts.
- Pitch national outlets with angle: "Pet-Loving Author Writes Cozy Mysteries That Warm the Heart."
- Guest posts on cozy blogs.

Events

- Launch party (online & in-person).
- Cozy-themed author panels at libraries.
- Virtual book club visits.

Promotions

- Goodreads giveaway.
- BookBub promotions (New Release + Featured Deal).
- Newsletter swaps with other cozy authors.

- Seasonal promotions tied to holidays (Halloween, Christmas).

Budget (Example)

- Cover design: $500
- Editing: $1,200
- ARC distribution (NetGalley): $450
- Facebook/Instagram Ads (3 months): $1,500
- BookBub Deal: $300–$600 (if approved)
- Launch party + giveaways: $300
- Total: ~$4,500

Success Metrics

- Amazon ranking in top 5,000 overall within launch week.
- 100+ reviews on Amazon and Goodreads within 90 days.
- 5,000 newsletter subscribers by end of year.
- Invitations to at least 3 book clubs or libraries for discussions.

Your marketing plan should be flexible—every author's audience and genre behave differently. Track results, double down on what works (ads, book clubs, social media platforms), and refine your approach for the next book.